THE TAN

Memories from a Romany Childhood

By

C J Smith

Grosvenor House
Publishing Limited

All rights reserved
Copyright © C J Smith, 2025

The right of C J Smith to be identified as the author of this
work has been asserted in accordance with Section 78
of the Copyright, Designs and Patents Act 1988

The book cover is copyright to C J Smith

This book is published by
Grosvenor House Publishing Ltd
Link House
140 The Broadway, Tolworth, Surrey, KT6 7HT.
www.grosvenorhousepublishing.co.uk

This book is sold subject to the conditions that it shall not, by way of
trade or otherwise, be lent, resold, hired out or otherwise circulated
without the author's or publisher's prior consent in any form of
binding or cover other than that in which it is published and
without a similar condition including this condition being
imposed on the subsequent purchaser.

A CIP record for this book
is available from the British Library

Paperback ISBN 978-1-83615-186-9
Hardback ISBN 978-1-83615-187-6

Preface: 'The Tan'

This memoir is about my life as a Romany Gypsy activist and my childhood awareness of a spiritual guide, that I refer to as, 'The man in the blue suit'. My story is predominantly set in the rural county of Herefordshire, in England, in the 1960s, 1970s, and 1980s, although it does move into my early and middle adulthood as far as the mid-2000s.

It explores the racism and prejudice that I and my family have endured and how we have overcome this, my colourful family history, my spiritual beliefs, and how I have lived my life as a gay Romany Gypsy in a culture that is traditionally seen (unfairly) by non-Gypsies, as intolerant towards homosexuality. This memoir challenges the myths and assumptions that society hold about our culture and tells how I and others are overcoming the prejudice and racism directed towards our communities.

The book describes my relationships with family members, and non-Gypsies and Travellers, my neighbours and friends, my school and education experiences, and early working life, including my career in management in the learning disabilities sector, along with a 30-year songwriting and performing role as a singer with my band 'The Brickshed'. I also explain how a series of tragic family events influenced my parents, my siblings, and me, and I describe my family history as far back as my great grandparents, in the 1800s.

This memoir tells how I have finally accepted that my spiritual experiences are indeed real and that my relationship with my guide, 'The man in the blue suit', is current and ongoing. I am a former manager of Travellers' Times, and I have written articles for newspapers that challenge the stereotypes portrayed by people in positions of power, and the media, about Gypsies and Travellers.

The book explains how my work in activism has been guided by 'The man in the blue suit' to provide Gypsy and Traveller Awareness training for: West Mercia Police Service, West Midlands CPS (Crime Prosecution Service) various local authorities and healthcare services, as well as several BBC production companies. I am currently working with The University of Worcester to produce and deliver Gypsy and Traveller Awareness training for healthcare students.

I wrote this book primarily as a record of sorts that we (Romany Gypsies) are present and productive members of the communities we live in, contributing to the diversity and success of every country we inhabit. Many people would like to see Gypsies and Travellers disappear from society, but we will always be here. We will adapt to change as we have always done, our culture will evolve, but it will continue to be guided by our heritage and history.

Now in my early sixties, I feel that my spiritual work, and my Gypsy and Traveller activism, is only just beginning. Our time is coming, and I am pleased to be part of our renaissance.

*Some parts of this memoir first appeared online on the Travellers' Times website in 2020.

C J Smith
November 2024

Dedications and Thanks

This book is dedicated to my two favourite uncles: my paternal uncle, Aldred (Aldy) Smith, for his patience, understanding, and unfailing kindness; and my maternal uncle, Thomas (Tommy) Smith, for keeping our family's stories alive, and taking the time to impart them to me.

Thanks also to the family and friends who have supported me throughout the writing process. You know who you are!

Reviews for 'The Tan'

What strikes me most, yet doesn't surprise me, is that even though the author was an academically bright child – he was placed into a 'slow' learner class when moving on to secondary education. A common experience across the UK, for many Romany children, was to be subjected to oppression in education, and this, in some part, is still in existence today.

What is a regular occurrence is the racism and discrimination that Gypsies and Travellers face within the state education system; the author shares with us his own struggles with this. The author writes: 'Unfortunately, little has changed, even today. Gypsies and Travellers are often asked to leave a school, when it is them who are the victims of racist attacks.'

The personal account of the author's family life and experiences I found fascinating, and this kept me hungry to turn the pages. In contrast to the stereotypes against our legitimate ethnicity-personal experience and diversity are just as widespread within our ethnic group, as to be found in any other ethnicity. Reading this book reminded me of this, because the author's life experiences are very different from my own. Yet, the similarities of having a hard-working ethos installed at an early age are just one of our shared traditions.

What is woven throughout this book are traditional family ties and the strength of a mother, who, despite her mental health issues, played a huge part in the author's life, and it is clear to see the strength of love between them. It is also impacting that the author's experiences of anxiety and fear, regarding his ethnic identity being known (during his childhood), is just one more account of what can be echoed again and again.

The author's career is one to be proud of! Especially when delivering the much needed cultural awareness training. This is an insightful and highly recommended must-read.

Gentylia Lee
Author of 'The Mystery in being a Gypsy'

Chris Smith presents the reader with a meticulously detailed account of his rural Herefordshire Gypsy family and community in a most balanced fashion. The tensions of a traditional community adapting to a rapidly modernising world are described in nostalgic, but realistic ways, telling it like it was and not over-romanticising the Gypsy life.

He convincingly depicts the tensions in traditional and contemporary Traveller life and this book will be of interest to local historians as well as a wider audience.

Overt and covert experiences of discrimination and loss are ever present throughout the book, which still manages to maintain an optimism about life. The communities' different responses to discrimination illustrates how one should never lump Gypsy and Traveller communities together, as they often hold quite differing beliefs and ways.

The book is very candid, and Chris does not 'sugar coat' any of the characters, including himself. The use of Gypsy language is also interspersed most effectively throughout, and I learnt a lot about how it must have been for his community, and doubtless many others.

A spiritual theme runs intriguingly throughout the book and the importance of this spirituality, and connection to the land, is woven throughout Chris's life and times, his work as a passionate advocate for his community continuing to the present day.'

Dr Peter Unwin
Principal Lecturer in Social Work
Research and Knowledge Exchange Co-ordinator
The University of Worcester.

The Tan

By C. J. Smith

Memory is a strange thing: I read, heard, or saw somewhere that what we really have are memories of memories. Memory is not stable: recollections come at different times, not in sequential order, but the strong ones stay with you. So it is with these.

* C J Smith, 2024

Chapter Titles

The Tan (Home, or The Place) 1
The Man in the Blue Suit 9
Beetles and Bumble Bees 12
The Sum of Injustice 14
The Red Shirt 19
Chirpy, Chirpy, Cheep, Cheep 24
Karmic Irony 30
The Cool Gang 35
Japes and Mistakes 43
Signs and Portents 49
Striving and Skiving 55
Prejudice and Party Games 61
Pocket Money and Pestilence 69
Love, Light, and Laurel and Hardy 75
Fairs and Thoroughfares 78
Presidential Premonitions 83
Storytelling Traditions 90
Daydreams and Dragonflies 94
Bells and Visitations 98
Copper Cans and Tin Churches 104
Life's Simple Pleasures 108
Soul Group Recollections 112
Furry Friends and Family Feuds 116
Swallows, Swifts, and Flights of Fancy 122
Fitting in and Tripping Out 127
Red Beads and Reading Wagons 131
Miracles and Milestones 133
Barton Street Theatre 137

Ridicule, Resentment, and Reassurance 142
The Twelve Apostles 146
Ravens and Revelations 152
Otherworldly Observations 161

Chapter One
The Tan

Mam and Dad bought their last vardo in 1947 from George Cox, a wheelwright and Gypsy wagon maker from Hereford, and it was decorated by Albert Wood in his beautiful, delicate, and distinctive style. Mr Cox was to become the last commercial vardo builder in Britain. Romany Gypsies from all over the land trusted him to build their homes, and his reputation was well-established and respected within the community. I missed out on the experience of living in the vardo, which Romanies described as an 'open lot', by a year. In 1960 Mam and Dad, like many other Romany Gypsies, decided to buy a caravan that we and most Romanies called a trailer. Many Gypsies were making this change due to the use of trucks and cars becoming commonplace. Trailers didn't require horses to move them, so people could travel from place to place much faster.

Our first trailer was an Eccles 20ft caravan. It looked fabulous and was part of the new wave of Gypsy culture. Although it looked great, both Mam and Dad bemoaned buying it. It was purchased, brand new, from Edmond's Caravans in Belmont Road, Hereford. The main issue was that it was damp. Mam and Dad returned it several times to have this defect rectified, but Mam had lost confidence in it and worried that it would make me (I was born a year after the purchase) sickly.

On a warm summer evening in 1963, my soon-to-be pregnant sister, Mary, and her husband, Bill, visited us. Mary was keen to tell Mam and Dad she had seen a Vickers trailer at Edmond's Caravans in Hereford. The trailer was just a year old, and she described it as beautiful inside and out. Vickers was the foremost maker of prestigious trailers aimed directly at the Gypsy and Traveller market.

The following Saturday, Mam, Dad, and my brother Len, with a two-year-old me in tow, went to see the trailer. The first question Mam asked Mrs Edmond, even before she inquired as to the price, was if anyone had died in the caravan. As she showed Mam to the trailer, Mrs Edmond reassured her that it had been sold due to the original purchasers inheriting property and not having space for the caravan. Mrs Edmond knew that it would be Mam who would decide whether or not to make the considerable investment. Vickers caravans cost more than an average house at the time due to their premier status in the Romany community. As soon as she stepped inside, Mam said she knew it was the home she wanted. The 22ft long beauty was cream, with a chestnut waistband, and it had multicoloured blinds at every window, even the one in the door, to keep the harsh sunlight out. Later years would see more flashy versions, with stainless steel bands, and engraved windows, but Mam did not hanker to trade for another, something inside telling her that this would be the last trailer she would own.

The inside was simply stunning: it was fitted with luxurious, patterned Axminster carpet and rich oak polished wooden units that blended superbly with pink and cream Formica in the kitchen area. High-quality, racing green, polished leather seating bunks, converted into two good-sized double beds, and large engraved mirrors augmented the perception of space and illumination. The trailer had full electrics: three round flush fitting, cut glass ceiling lights were strategically placed in a line centrally, along with flower engraved, diffused side wall lamps. There was a full-sized white and stainless-steel gas cooker and matching electric larder fridge. Mam never used the cooker; throughout the years, it always retained its brand-new appearance and was cleaned until it glistened on a weekly basis. An enamelled Parkray double-door stove with glass inserts was set in a mosaic tile surround, which shone like jewels. This made the trailer blisteringly warm, and early in the evening, it had to be allowed to die down in order for us to sleep comfortably.

The Vickers was Mam's pride and joy, and the aroma of beeswax furniture polish enveloped the senses as you entered the trailer. Every surface gleamed and glimmered. The glass display cupboards were filled with expensive Crown Derby, Ainsley crockery, and cut-glass vases and baskets. None of these display items were ever used to eat or drink off, and the cups at no time held tea, but they were washed until they sparkled with loving regularity. Mam didn't use the cooker in the trailer because she disliked cooking smells that invaded the sleeping area. Sleeping, or receiving visitors, was what the Vickers was primarily used for. In my teenage years, I was allowed to listen to music in the trailer, but no dancing was permitted for fear that a Crown Derby plate might be dislodged and broken, ruining the set and garnering my mother's ire.

Our main living area was a shed—a corrugated tin shed, to be precise. The shed was part of a small row that had originally been used to accommodate hop and fruit pickers in the seasons. Dad converted the two end units nearest the trailer into one; he lined the inside with plasterboard to ensure warmth and a smooth surface, onto which Mam pasted gaudy orange and brown psychedelic wallpaper.

The owner of the farm where we lived adapted the other sheds in the row to provide flush toilets and a 'water shed' containing a large Belfast sink with big brass taps, wooden draining boards, and storage cupboards. The shed had no windows to let in natural light, but this hardly mattered as the door was almost always open, weather permitting. It did have electricity, however, ensuring that we had light in the evening and power for the television. It was heated, first, by a black-lead stove, and later by a double oven Rayburn that Mam used to cook with before acquiring a Calor gas cooker, the Rayburn then being utilised for heating only, unless the gas bottle ran out unexpectedly. The cream-coloured Rayburn was placed to the right of the door, opposite a heavily laden, square table, which was covered with one of a selection of brightly patterned tablecloths that hung almost to floor level, obscuring the boxes of crockery and tinned food underneath. Four wooden kitchen chairs with padded seats surrounded the table. Mam and Dad also managed to fit in a black vinyl settee with orange seat covers and an easy chair with wood arms that Dad liked to use. Mam had a variety of woollen rugs of different sizes covering the whole floor space.

All around us was greenery. Directly opposite our tan was a large mature apple orchard, and across the quiet byway was a hop garden that extended alongside the whole length of the roadway from the tan to the main road, half a mile away. Birds, butterflies, and all manner of flying insects were abundant, along with hedgehogs and many other mammals that fascinated and intrigued me. Rats, though, could not be endured, and if they were foolish enough to come near, they were quickly dispatched with poison or by our cats and dogs.

Whenever a gorja visited our tan, Mam usually invited them into the Vickers trailer. We rented a field for our horses from Mr Zeuner, a neighbour and the science teacher at Canon Frome Secondary School that I attended. When he came to tell us one evening that one of our mares had given birth to a foal in his field, Mam invited him into the trailer. I was sat on one of the bunks, fortuitously doing my homework. As he stepped inside, his jaw dropped in awe at the luxury of our home. His eyes slowly took in the luxurious fixtures and fittings, and he gasped in amazement before saying to Mam, "Mrs Smith, you have a beautiful home." Mam smiled and thanked him for the compliment. "Anyone would be proud to live in this caravan," he continued. This, of course, was precisely the reaction that Mam was looking for. She enjoyed bucking the expectations of gorjas, who often considered Romany people to be poor and dirty because we didn't live in housing.

Some Gypsies were poor, but many were not. Romanies with large families worked alongside each other and pooled their money to ensure that they could afford the best vehicles and trailers. We were always well dressed and well fed. Many Gypsies and Travellers had no rent or mortgages to find money for and were able to save in a way that house dwellers could only dream of. Romanies hardly ever bought items on the 'never-never' as Mam and Dad referred to credit, as this was frowned on in our culture. Also, many Gypsies had no fixed address and therefore did not qualify for loans anyway.

The summer of 1976 was one of the hottest on record. The United Kingdom experienced ten consecutive weeks of uninterrupted sunshine, causing a significant drought, with water being rationed across the country. Farmers, however, were allowed to irrigate their crops, often-times taking the water directly from local rivers until many nearly ran dry. We lived near the river Frome, a beautiful stretch of water that meandered through some stunning countryside, which, as a child, I took for granted, never having lived anywhere else. I didn't always appreciate being brought up in a rural community. Towns and cities held a fascination due to the number of people they had. I found it hard to imagine that anyone could ever be bored if they lived in a city. Rural life was much slower; time ticked by, especially on weekends.

What I remember most about Sunday mornings is waking up to the smell of kippers frying in the pan. I would lie in bed until the last moment before Mam insisted that it was time to get up. After a late breakfast, Dad, Uncle Aldy, and my brother Len would go to the pub, leaving Mam to cook the dinner and me to play my ever-growing record collection or listen to Ed 'Stewpot' Stewart on the radio. 'Mississippi', by Pussycat, was one of the summer's big hits. It seemed to be playing pretty much constantly, along with 'Save Your Kisses for Me' by Brotherhood of Man, which had won the Eurovision Song Contest a couple of months earlier. 'Save your Kisses' had a neat little dance that went with it, which everyone seemed to know, and I practised to perfection.

One of the ways a teenager could earn money was through fruit picking. Yarkhill Farm grew strawberries and black currents in abundance. Many other Gypsy families stopped on the farm between June and the end of September. They would arrive for the strawberry picking, and most would stay until the hops were harvested. I liked picking blackcurrants and was good at it. My only concern being whether I had earned enough money to go into Hereford on Saturdays and buy another record. It was during this period that I realised I could sing. I would sing the hits of the day to keep amused whilst picking. Often this would turn into a competition with many of the chavvies from the other Gypsy families, some of whom could also sing well.

Joannie Lee, a large Romany woman who could work as hard as any man, said to Mam one day as they were queuing for the weighing scales, "Your boy can really sing Betty, and he knows how to get the meaning of a song across." Mam glowed with pride, as always, if one of her children was complimented. The Lee Family, along with the Boswells and our relatives, the Johns Family from Evesham, were regular visitors to Yarkhill Farm for the picking season. Most of the farms in the area received and welcomed Romany Gypsies during this time. Romanies comprised most of the labour pool, and we were valued due to our work ethic. The same families returned to the same farms year after year and were accepted and mostly respected by the locals.

As summer drifted almost imperceptibly into autumn, hop-picking began in earnest. Mam didn't enjoy working in the deafening hop-picking machine shed, preferring instead to be in the relatively peaceful hop garden out in the fresh air. She would mainly be on the back of the hop trailer, laying the scratchy bines neatly in the trailer, working side by side with Dad. Hop harvesting usually began straight after the late August bank holiday and would last approximately six weeks. Fuggles, Northdown, Golding, and Challenger hops were the main varieties that were grown in Herefordshire.

My brother Len worked in the hop drying kilns, which were hot and stuffy and had an overwhelming, almost demonic aroma due to the sulphur used in the drying process. The job was tough, and they had to work through the night to keep up with the pickers, catching a few broken hours of sleep when they could during the day. Len went on to become one of the best-known hop dryers in the country, winning many awards.

Clive Bennett, a tall, slim man with a shock of unruly red hair, worked in the crow's nest, a metal construction lifted and attached to the back of the trailer. Clive would climb up inside the crow's nest and cut the hop-bines from the top, enabling Mam and Dad to pull them into the trailer. Mam would occasionally take a break from this arduous work to walk behind the tractor and trailer, picking up 'flags' that were actually hop sprays that had fallen to the ground.

One day, Clive, whilst chopping a particularly resistant hop bine ('bine' being the correct word, and not as most people think, a hop 'vine'), lost his grip on the extremely sharp hook he used, and it went spinning out of his hand towards Mam. She was bending down at the time and didn't see it coming. Fortunately, it was the wooden handle that struck her on the head and knocked her out briefly. Had it been the blade, she probably wouldn't have been around to tell the tale later.

My favourite time after the picking day was over was the early evening. The workers would gather around an iron grate that stood raised on metal legs and was known as a 'devil'. Ghost stories would be told in the fading light, extending well into the darkness, with only flames from the 'Devil's' fire to illuminate the faces of the people there. I would sit and listen quietly as the pickers told tales that sometimes stretched the imagination, although they often had a ring of truth about them. I would frequently be too trashed ('trashed' being our word for scared or afraid) to walk back to our trailer by myself, choosing instead to wait until another member of the group headed in the right direction.

Most years during this time, we were visited by Pakistani and Indian men selling brightly coloured blankets, throws, and tablecloths out of the back of their cars or vans. They did a lot of business with the Romany people, and their goods were exceptionally well made. One afternoon, an extremely handsome Pakistani man and his wife arrived at our tan. As he opened up the back of his car for us to peruse his goods, he asked Mam politely for a drink of water for his heavily pregnant wife, who was sitting in the front passenger seat. Mam looked at me, and said, "Jel akie and get the Moosh some parnie."

The man's face immediately lit up with a brilliant smile, and he said: "You speak our tongue!" He went on to say that our people and his must have a similar heritage, as we shared many words in our languages. It was the first time I realised that we had a history that was not widely known at the time. Mam bought several of the blankets that I still have and use, and they look as good today as they did all those years ago.

When we were at home, my family usually spoke the 'Poggadi jib', which translates to 'the broken language'. This is a mixture of English and traditional Romany. The Romany language evolved over hundreds of years and uses words from Sanskrit, Dardic, Burushaski, Persian, Kurdish, and Ossetian, to name a few. English verbs are combined with Romany words to produce our unique vocabulary. Many words currently in English are of Romany extraction, although most people who use terms like 'Kushty', 'Vonga', and 'Cosh' don't realise this.

Mam and Dad used the Romany language more than I or my siblings did, as we had more influence from school and from increased contact with gorjas. However, my parents continued to learn new English words, and it always amused me when I heard them use a word or phrase unaccustomed to them for the first time. When my mother started using 'apparently' in her sentences, I was encouraged to know that she could still grasp an understanding of new (to her) words. She did not always get this right, however; a common saying in the 1970s due to the emergence of the TV show 'The Bionic Man' starring Lee Majors was, 'I'm not bionic, you know' if someone was asked to do something too quickly, for example. My mother either misheard or misunderstood this and would say instead, 'I'm not antibiotic, you know!' My family and I found this hilarious, but we never corrected her; we just enjoyed her misspeak.

Chapter Two

The Man in the Blue Suit

My first memory, more of an impression of pictures on an old-time projector, is of tipping my pram over. I liked to bounce while in the pram, often whilst listening to the radio at the same time as sucking on a bottle of milk. I was parked at the end of a strawberry row. Mam and my sister Mary, who was radiant and just married at the age of twenty-two, were gradually getting closer, picking slowly towards the pram that I was happily bouncing in. I was nearly two years old the day I jumped backwards, causing the Silver Cross model to flip into the air and land on top of me. I was lying in the dirt looking through the gap under the pram and could see my sister and mother running towards me. My sister, being younger, reached me first and hoisted the perambulator, shiny, sturdy, and strong, from off of me. As she looked down and Mam arrived looking panicked, I sat up and laughed loudly. My sister smiled at me and said, "He's alright; it might teach him a lesson about bouncing." It didn't.

The day, a year later, that I first saw and spoke with the man wearing the blue suit and trilby hat, I was enjoyably ensconced, playing on the muddy headland at the edge of the hop garden. It must have been near picking time because the rich scent of almost ripe hops in the late summer sun enveloped me, and the large leaves created a dappled effect around me. The man spoke in a rich, deep, and friendly voice, whereupon I looked up to see him sitting about fifteen feet above me on the nearby telegraph wires, his legs dangling in the air. This didn't seem remarkable or frightening to me in any way. It was as if he'd always been in my life. Even though it was our first encounter, I recognised him and instantly discerned that he knew me. He asked me how I was feeling, and I replied affirmatively, although, at just that moment, I noticed a slight discomfort in my belly. He smiled warmly and said to tell my mother and father to take me to the hospital without delay. He informed me that I would be spending some time away from home, but that I shouldn't be afraid as everything was going to be alright. I glanced down at my belly, giving it a rub, and when I looked up again, he had vanished.

I did as he asked. I'm sure my parents were sceptical or doubtful, but that's not how I remember it. My recollection of it is that they didn't hesitate in believing me. With the pain in my stomach growing feverishly, my brother Len, who had recently passed his driving test, was dispatched to get the motor ready. Mam warned me that it was best not to tell the doctor about the man in blue. She didn't elaborate on this, though.

I'm unsure of how long I spent in Hereford Hospital; however, I know that I had to spend six weeks recuperating at St. Mary's in Burghill, Herefordshire. Gastroenteritis was a severe illness for a small child in the early sixties, and St. Mary's, at that time, was used as a convalescence hospital. Mam rode with me in the ambulance from Hereford County, with Dad and Uncle Aldy following behind in my uncle's van.

I cried when they had to leave and was only consoled by the teddy bear my uncle had bought for me. I kept that bear until well into adulthood, not having the heart to part with it. The nurses were wonderful and wore fashionable 1960s uniforms topped off with tiny round pillbox hats. Most of the building was occupied by adults, with only three or four children in our ward; each of us was separated by half-glass walls so that we could see each other but not touch or interact physically. The staff spent many hours with us, ensuring that we were happy and comfortable. I was the youngest child, and as I grew stronger, I was allowed to follow the nurses around while they completed their daily tasks. The place I loved best was the laundry room—a vast space filled to the ceiling with varying sizes of cane laundry baskets.

Matrons were still firmly in charge of hospital wards, and one pretty, young nurse was not keen on the starchy matron at all. She persuaded me to hide in one of the baskets and to jump up and roar loudly when Matron passed by. When I did this, the matron was shocked and annoyed and shouted sharply at me. The nurse, who had encouraged me, rushed in and scooped me up, saying to the matron that 'boys will be boys' and then carried me to the kitchen for ice cream, humming a popular Cliff Richard tune and smiling with a gleeful spring in her step.

I saw and spoke with the man in blue several times in the intervening years before I began primary school and on the odd time after. Sometimes, I told Mam and Dad about these encounters; often, I didn't. It was no big deal to me, and it appeared perfectly normal, in fact. For many years, I thought little about the man in blue, and he figured in my life only infrequently. When I was well into adulthood, he entered my world again, although I don't think there was ever a time when he wasn't around.

Chapter Three
Beetles and Bumble Bees

Growing up in the heart of the Herefordshire countryside in the 1960s and 70s meant being close to nature and observing the passing seasons. Mam worked on the land and would take me along until I started school and during the holidays after. I adored being in the fields, searching for beetles, and shouting "beet, beet!" excitedly when I discovered one. My family has always had an affinity with animals. We had chickens, dogs, cats, and horses. I even kept mice for a while until they inevitably escaped. Mam was not happy about this. I had stick insects for quite a few years as well, which I found fascinating. I loved the way they could be indistinguishable from their surroundings. I liked to be invisible too sometimes, and I would often sit under the table that was covered with a long tablecloth and secretly listen to the adults talking. This could be a bit embarrassing for my parents if I repeated what I'd heard later, and I soon learned not to do this, even when I overheard something I didn't understand.

Mam always took me with her when she visited our relatives in Evesham. Aunt Mimey and Uncle Nelson lived in a house close to the hospital near the centre of the town. We caught the bus from Tarrington and made the 90-minute journey several times a year. I loved accompanying Mam on these excursions. At the back of Aunt Mimey's house was a large covered market, where I spent many hours browsing around the various stalls. When I was a teenager, I was allowed to go alone, and I spent a large part of the summer holidays with my aunt and uncle and working alongside my cousins. One of the primary jobs during the spring and summer months was onion pulling. My cousin Neil had a talent for this work and could pull twice as many as me. The worst part about working in the onion patch was the smell. You didn't notice it much in the fields, but when the working day was over, and we arrived home, the rancid aroma was infused into our clothing and skin.

No matter how much you scrubbed your hands, it would never altogether remove the smell, which could linger for weeks afterwards.

I have very few regrets about my childhood, but one thing still haunts me. Mam and her friend, Mrs Scott, were hoeing weeds in the strawberry fields alongside many other women who had been brought in by bus and were known as 'The Mordifords', eponymously named after the village where they lived. I was about ten years old and had spent most of the day fishing for minnows in a brook with a net and jam jar Mrs Scott had brought me. At the end of the dinner break, I was sent to 'Pop Harford's' to buy a few sundry items, including fly spray. 'Pop's' was our nearest shop, and it was easy to get to across the fields. As I left the shop and walked down the lane, I bumped into some gorja kids with whom I was acquainted; they were a couple of years older than me. I was keen to fit in and be accepted, and I was pleased when they stopped to talk with me.

One of the older boys noticed a bumble bee busily gathering nectar on a nearby flower plant and, in a sly and goading manner, encouraged me to kill it with the fly spray. I really didn't want to do this, knowing in my soul that it was wrong. Peer pressure at a young age can be crushing, though, and the older boys were chanting, "Do it, do it", so, reluctantly, I sprayed the insect. As the other boys cheered and whooped, I experienced an overwhelming feeling of guilt and shame for inflicting pain and suffering onto an innocent creature. Tears welled up in me as I watched the bee struggle for breath, and I slowly backed away, horrified at what I'd done. I ran from the other kids back towards where Mam was working, with the sound of their derisive laughter ringing in my ears.

When I told Mam and Mrs Scott what had happened, they comforted me, using soothing tones, and then Mam, placing her hands on my shoulders, and looking lovingly into my tear-filled eyes, said, "Never let anyone make you do something that you know is wrong." The incident taught me not to be influenced in such a way again. Since that day, I have never harmed another living creature. Now, I collect spiders or wasps and carefully place them outside if needed. I learned to follow my own path and to listen to my inner voice. The guilt of what I did is still with me, though. I think it always will be.

Chapter Four
The Sum of Injustice

My relationship with my mother, Elizabeth (Betty for short), although a loving one, was nonetheless demanding, almost from my earliest memories. Mam was overprotective; some might say controlling. I realise now that this was somewhat understandable, considering that she had lost both of her full-blood brothers in tragic circumstances, and she worried about my safety as her youngest child in an almost obsessive way.

I was nearly five years old the day my mother discovered her younger brother Joe had been killed in a street fight. It was a warm late spring afternoon when two policemen approached our tan. One was wearing civvies, and the other was in uniform. I didn't hear what they said, but I vividly recall her reaction. She placed her left hand above her temple and screamed, not the sort of scream you hear in Hammer House of Horror movies, but a visceral howl filled with grief and longing for this news to be erroneous.

My father and older brother were at work, and I knew that Mam needed someone's support other than mine and the police officers. It was probably fear and concern that made me run across the village green to our neighbour, Mrs Oliver's, house – or maybe I just needed to escape the lamenting sound of my mother's pain. Mrs Oliver carried me back to our tan and spoke quietly to the gavvers before doing her best to comfort Mam, who was now walking in circles and slapping her chest, head, and legs whilst moaning and crying uncontrollably.

This memory is embedded within me, as is the fact that the following day, my mother had a streak of pure white hair above her left temple where she had placed her hand the day before. This 'Mallen Streak' stayed with her for the remainder of her life and served as a permanent, conspicuous reminder of the events of that day in 1966. Mental health issues plagued Mam for a number of years following this latest of tragedies, culminating in her having breakdowns that persisted during my early childhood. Even as a preschool child, I was aware of my mother's torment and would try to alleviate it by taking her hand and walking with her through the countryside, attempting to distract her with the beauty of our surroundings. Yet her grief was all-enveloping and clouded every aspect of our lives.

To cushion myself from the effects of Mam's melancholy, I withdrew into the world of television, books, and music. I became immersed in programmes such as 'White Horses', 'Belle and Sebastian', 'Champion the Wonder Horse' and 'Casey Jones'. I can still evoke the theme tunes of these shows with perfect clarity. My favourites were 'Batman', 'Star Trek', and 'Doctor Who'. Fantasy, space, and time fascinated me and still do to this day. All of these series had one overriding theme: the triumph of right over wrong. Children of my generation were lucky to have the difference between good and bad instilled within us from various sources: parents, school, television and books, to name a few. Unfairness of any kind affected me deeply.

Hardly anything lingers in your memory as much as a feeling of injustice. I began my school life at the age of five at the village primary school in Yarkhill, Herefordshire. I recall only two teachers, although there may have been more that have been lost from my recollection over the intervening years: Miss Preece, the headmistress, and Mrs Pitt, who taught most of our lessons.

The walk to school lasted half an hour, and the village's parents took turns escorting us kids each morning and afternoon. I always preferred it when Mrs Beebee was the escort. She encouraged us to store our school shoes in our bags and to wear our wellingtons, allowing us to walk in the brook when the water wasn't too deep in the spring and summer months. I loved the smell and feel of catkins brushing my face from the overhanging trees.

I was a quick learner, quicker than most of my classmates, and consequently finished my work before the other kids my age. So, I would often be admonished by Mrs Pitt for staring out of the windows wistfully, longingly waiting for the school bell to ring so that I could begin the journey home. For some reason, the fact that I found the lessons easy seemed to infuriate Mrs Pitt, and she appeared to enjoy calling me out to the front of the class on the occasions that I made a mistake in my work. If I did make an error, it was usually in a math lesson and almost invariably because I had misread a question, but I could also be easily distracted by one of my classmates.

On this particular day, after handing in my work first, Mrs Pitt looked pleased that she had an opportunity to call me to the front of the class and exclaim that I had done my sums wrong. I was told off while everyone watched, and she took a long wooden ruler out of her desk drawer. She held my left hand out before her and smacked it hard several times with the ruler. I bit my lip and tried not to show any emotion as tears welled in my eyes. She then glanced at my workbook again, and a look of surprise and disappointment crossed her face as she said, "Oh, you have got it right!" She then looked me in the eyes, and I observed an expression of shame cross her features before she dismissively said, "Well, those smacks will have to do for another day." I walked slowly, without saying a word, back to my desk, rubbing my hand, which was red and stinging with pain. I just couldn't comprehend why she hadn't apologised to me for her error.

After that experience, I made sure to take more time over my work, even though I didn't need it, to ensure Mrs Pitt never had an opportunity to treat me in such a manner again. I learned a lesson that day, but doubtless not the one that the teacher intended.

Mam's depression came and went depending on the time of year, the onset of autumn, especially the clocks going back, triggering a bleak dolefulness that would not end until spring lifted the veil of winter darkness. I've often wondered, as an adult, if Mam suffered from a form of seasonal affective disorder, but I think it was more than that. The loss of her brothers weighed heavily on her heart. It was the kind of sadness that could not be alleviated by discussing it, and it gave no respite once it overwhelmed her. She tried to hide it from us but was always unsuccessful in her attempts. I would catch a faraway look in her bright blue eyes, a look that said everything was somehow spoiled, tainted with a sourness that only she could taste. Spring and summer months were usually different. Her mood would lift as her eyes sparkled with hope again. She would look at me with pride and happiness, and I loved to catch even a glimpse of that look. It meant everything to me. The lighter side of Mam's personality would come to the fore, and the world and every aspect of it took on a brighter hue.

She could be funny, engaging, and defiant in turns. Mam loved going to work on the land. She was industrious and, even in her seventies, could toil as hard as women half her age. She was valued by the local farmers for her work ethic and honesty. Mam was a trusted employee who enjoyed being in the company of other like-minded women, laughing and joking during the long and often arduous day. Land work was seasonal, and when it wasn't available, Mam would go out calling, sometimes known as hawking. She sold paper and wooden flowers made by my father, lucky charms, and lace. The flowers had to be of good quality. Mam would sneer at my father and dismiss any she considered not up to scratch for her to sell.

She had a warm, inviting, beautiful smile that could disarm the most prejudiced of people. Emotional intelligence figured highly in her makeup. She was perceptive, and this helped enormously when she was often asked to tell someone's fortune. She could intuit easily what the person needed to hear. She was also easily hurt or offended by an offhand remark and would respond by either withdrawing or going on the attack. Mam had a temper and was not afraid to pogger (hit) someone if she felt it was required to defend herself or her family.

One Saturday afternoon in the 1950s, my grandmother was struck by a police officer whilst he was attempting to break up an altercation between Granny Rose and some other Romany women at the bus station in Hereford. The officer's helmet was knocked off by granny, resulting in him punching her, and Mam did not hesitate for a second to wade in to defend her stepmother, culminating in them both being arrested and charged with affray.

Chapter Five
The Red Shirt

Mam's best friend was a gorja. I loved Doreen Scott and her partner Clive. They were warm, kind-hearted people who lived without prejudice, and I learned from a young age that not all gorjas viewed Gypsies with suspicion and hate. Indeed, because we lived in a small village and worked on the land, we had no choice but to take people at face value, as most of our fellow workers (outside of hop and fruit picking) were country people. Mrs Scott always gave me gifts at Christmas and birthdays. They were presents that fed my imagination and assisted my learning. She recognised that I had an inquiring mind and encouraged me to follow my interests. Mam and Dad were keen for me to do well in education, too. In particular, Dad recognised that the world was changing, and most of the jobs that Romanies had traditionally done would no longer exist in an increasingly mechanised world.

Doreen and Clive were responsible for giving me my first excursion to the seaside. Mrs Scott arranged a day trip, booked a bus, and ensured that most of the kids and parents from our village were on board. Ironically, the Scott's were Welsh, and Mam had been born in Nantyglo, so they had a natural affinity with resorts such as Barry and Porthcawl in South Wales. I liked making sandcastles on the beach but loved the fairground rides more. The excitement of going on the Big Dipper was tremendous. The thrill and speed were like nothing that I had known before, and Clive would say, "He had his eyes closed for most of the ride", so we would stay on and go around again with Clive urging me to keep my eyes open this time so that I got the whole experience.

The old saying goes that 'pride comes before a fall', but I think it depends on what or whom you're proud of. I wanted my parents to feel a sense of pride when they spoke about me. One of the ways I could achieve this was through doing well at school. My first primary school in Yarkhill closed in August 1969 when I was eight years old, and I began the new term that September at Withington County Primary School. Our village's small band of kids shared the same taxi to Withington Primary School. The taxi was a black London-style cab driven by a genuinely lovely man, Mr Harmer.

I enjoyed Mr Harmer's company, as he had exciting stories to tell on the journeys to and from school, and it made us kids feel exceptional riding in the back of the unusual vehicle. Mr Harmer was knowledgeable about many things, and he sometimes spoke about the racism and prejudice that many Black and Asian people experienced, expressing sadness that some people could be so cruel. Enoch Powell had made his 'Rivers of Blood' speech a year earlier, and race riots across the country followed this. I think Mr Harmer was aware that many Gypsies and Travellers were subjected to prejudice and racism, too, as he was always thoughtful towards me and enjoyed speaking with Mam and Dad whenever he saw them.

During that time, the headmaster of Withington School was Mr Edwards. He treated us Gypsy kids no differently from the gorja children, and he recognised my academic ability and especially my love of books and literature straight away. He was an excellent narrator and enjoyed bringing alive novels such as 'The Borrowers' and my personal favourite, 'The Weirdstone of Brisingamen' by Alan Garner, a book that I have read many times, even as an adult.

One of the highlights of the school year was the nativity play. We Romanies didn't usually get offered any of the major acting parts, and we had learned from experiences at our previous school not to expect too much. During one lunchtime break, as I walked past the staff room door, I overheard a heated debate going on inside about who should be the narrator of the play. The narrator's role was the plum part, and there was quite a bit of competition for it. Through the closed door, I clearly heard Mr Edwards say, "I don't care about that; he's the best reader, and he can give it the gravitas that it deserves." I wasn't sure what gravitas meant and had to look it up in the dictionary. Later that day, Mr Edwards took me to one side and asked if I would take on the role, and I agreed immediately.

I practised for many hours leading up to the first performance to ensure I was word perfect. Mam and Mrs Scott attended the first night and chose seats in the front row. I was the only child on stage for the whole play, standing on a wooden box behind a podium, stage right so that the entire audience could see me. Thankfully, the preparation paid off, and I read with authority and confidence, and I will never forget the expressions of relief on my mother's and Mrs Scott's faces. At the end of the performance, Mam had tears in her eyes, and Mrs Scott stood up and led the applause; both were beaming with pride. I will be forever grateful to Mr Edwards for giving me that opportunity; in fact, he played a large part in instilling self-belief and self-confidence within me. Whenever I walk onto a stage now, whether delivering Gypsy and Traveller awareness training to the Police, The Crown Prosecution Service, the NHS, or as a singer with my band, The Brickshed, I often think of him and inwardly thank him for being the exceptional teacher he was.

Mam and Dad's relationship was undoubtedly built on love, but as with all unions, was not without its tribulations. Dad's brother, Uncle Dick, had been one of the men who had been drinking with Mam's brother, Uncle Mushy, the night he died. Due to the circumstances of his death, there was much speculation about what actually occurred. Mam believed that Dad's brother and the others present on that fateful night knew more than they said. Whenever Uncle Dick's name was mentioned, she would raise her eyebrows and turn her head away, indicating that she didn't wish to discuss him. However, I think she agreed to attend his wedding for the sake of keeping the peace. Uncle Dick's marriage in 1970 was the first wedding that I attended. He married Rhoda, a widow with two daughters slightly older than me.

I felt a little special as my buttonhole flower was a red carnation; everyone else wore white carnations or roses. I delighted in standing out from the crowd.

An example happened at Withington Primary School, where the centenary and Thanksgiving photographs were taken a few years later. The older boys, like me, had been instructed to wear white shirts for the photo, which would appear in the local newspaper. On the day, though, I neglected to tell my mother this and turned up in a red shirt. My cousin Michael, who is the same age as me, was fuming, declaring, "You just wore that shirt to be different." I denied this and said I'd simply forgotten the white shirt instruction. This was a lie. I wanted to be seen.

I didn't know Granddad Sam well as he died when I was three in September 1964. My dad's family came from Gloucestershire. They travelled and stopped around Cinderford, Coleford, and Lydney in the Forest of Dean before moving to Herefordshire at the end of The First World War, where my grandfather had served. He would serve in the Second World War, also as a rifleman. Granny Ada collected me granddad's war pension, which only amounted to a few shillings per week, from the local post office a couple of miles away. The postmaster gave her two weeks' worth of money at a time to save her walking there every week. After my granddad died, she received a stern letter from the War Pensions Office demanding the return of one week's worth of his pension. The letter stated that she would be taken to court if it wasn't repaid immediately. When she showed the postmaster the letter, he was so incensed that he wrote to the War Pension Department chastising them for harassing a widow for such a paltry sum, considering that her husband had served in two world wars. Granny repaid the money.

Granddad Sam was canny. He purchased property and land in Withington near Hereford, which was the family home, but he never lived there himself. Instead, he chose to stay in his wagon on the farm at Shawle Court. He rented out the property and land, providing a decent income for himself and his family whilst living rent-free and working for the Barnes family in Monkhide, Herefordshire. It took around forty minutes to walk to Granny's tan from our place in Yarkhill. I made this journey many times, walking across the fields and through the lanes to get there. I often went with Granny Ada and my aunts

Louise and Mary to collect water from the well just down the road, carrying enamelled buckets that were considerably heavier when filled with water on the return journey. The well water was pure and sweet and exceedingly cold, always a boon on a hot summer's day.

Granny Ada loved Neapolitan ice cream and would often send me to the village shop to buy it for her, happily sharing it when I returned. When my Uncle Dick had a serious car accident a year after getting married, Granny was devastated, and Uncle Dick never really recovered. He died in March 1974 from a brain tumour. I loved my Granny Ada very much and was heartbroken when she passed five months later in September that same year. Uncle Dick would reappear in my life many years after his passing.

In the mid-2000s a friend of mine, Alison Jennings, who I appeared with in many stage musicals, including 'Oliver!' where I played Bill Sykes opposite her as Nancy, invited me to a spiritualist evening at the Prince of Wales Inn, Ross-on-Wye. Intrigued, I agreed to attend with her. We sat in a circle and listened carefully as various group members received messages, some more successfully than others. Just as the meeting ended, the medium suddenly looked at me and said, "There is a man here who wants to speak with you."

Alison and I looked at each other as the woman in her late thirties stepped towards me. She then told me that the man's name was Richard and that he was telling her that when I was a small boy, I would lick the cream from the tops of milk bottles but leave the milk. I agreed that it was true. Alison asked me if I knew a man called Richard; I said, "Yes, he was my uncle, but we called him Dick."

The medium then said that he was asking her to tell me to keep an eye on the tyre pressure on my car and that he often dropped in to see how I was doing. When we got outside, we walked around my car and visually checked the tyres, which all looked fine. Afterward we went for a drink in Ross, discussing the evening's events. The milk statement had perplexed me with its accuracy.

The next morning, as I left home and walked towards my car to go to work, I immediately saw that one of the front tyres was completely flat. I was confounded but somehow not surprised or even anxious. In fact, I was pleased that my uncle appeared to be visiting me.

Chapter Six
Chirpy, Chirpy, Cheep, Cheep

My dad, Leonard Smith, enjoyed the simple pleasures of life. He was an introvert who was grateful for good food, a warm trailer, the love of his family, and a peaceful existence. He was not brash or lairy, but he was clever. He could do sums in his head that many couldn't do with a calculator nowadays. He also taught himself to read and write, and although his spelling wasn't great, his understanding was. He was a thinker who didn't mind his own company and was certainly no pushover. At his core, he was a decent, moral man who felt emotions deeply without needing to make a song and dance of things. He only had a handful of friends, yet they would have died for him, if necessary. His best friend was his brother-in-law, my Uncle Mushy, whose death before I was born became a kind of legend in our family lore and who Dad spoke of so often that I felt I knew him too.

Our tan was on the edge of the village green, and we lived there for over twenty years in Yarkhill, Herefordshire. Mam and my brother were employed on the farm where we lived, and Dad worked on the next farm over at Shawle Court, Monkhide, alongside four of his brothers and sisters. Dad always wore a flat cap, even though he had a great head of hair right up until he passed over in February 2009 at the age of 91.

He also carried a walking stick; he didn't need one, but it was his weapon of choice if there was ever a need to defend himself or his family.

He was good with horses and kept chickens, too; they weren't caged in a coop, instead he let them roam freely, and we kids enjoyed spending hours searching for the nests of eggs. Some hens always evaded us, though, and on a Sunday morning in the summer of 1970, a hen appeared with ten chicks. Every time Dad walked near her or the chicks, the hen would puff up her feathers and fly at him, pecking his legs. My brother and I were watching from the trailer window when we saw Dad finally lose patience with the bad-tempered bird, and he tapped her lightly on the head with his stick. The hen immediately fell to the floor, and my brother exclaimed, "Oh dordy, me dad's mullered the hen". We then watched open-mouthed as Dad dropped onto one knee, took his hat off, and frantically started to waft his cap back and forth over the bird's head. Whereupon the hen stood up, looking a bit dazed, before making off with her chicks in tow. Dad looked extremely relieved that he didn't have ten orphaned chicks to look after, and the hen left him alone after that.

As he walked back into the trailer, in a moment of synchronicity, 'Chirpy Chirpy Cheep Cheep', a popular song by the pop group Middle of the Road, began playing on the radio. My brother and I started to sing along, "Where's your mama gone, where's your mama gone, far, far, away?" and then fell about laughing. Dad looked at us like we were divvies (fools) though he couldn't help but chuckle too.

Saturdays were exciting because it meant a trip to Hereford to do the weekly shop. Mam and I would catch the bus that ran twice a week, Wednesday (market day) and Saturday. Sometimes, after my brother passed his driving test and got a vehicle, he would drive us. Still, as he got older, he often had his own agenda, which usually involved going to the pub and meeting girls. Afterwards, he would drive home when the pubs shut, late afternoon, much the worse for wear, in a time before breathalysers, when thankfully and fortuitously; there were far fewer vehicles on the roads.

Chadd's of Hereford was a fabulous department store based in Commercial Street. It was my favourite place to shop. If what you needed couldn't be found on one of the four packed floors, then it probably wasn't worth having. The toy section in the basement was every child's dream, and I spent many hours exploring there. It was the place to go and had the best selection of Dinky toys that I have ever seen. Cars of various sizes made from different metals and plastics were abundant, along with Batman toys, games, and costumes. Meccano, Etch-a-Sketch, Chopper bikes, Scooters, and Evel Knievel stunt cycles were placed at strategic points to catch the eye; dolls and teddy bears, including my personal favourite Rupert, were among a myriad of other desirable items. The department also included every board game imaginable, making the eyes of children and adults alike alight with pleasure.

The record department was the best in the city, and the staff were both knowledgeable and helpful. As a teenager, I spent many hours flipping through the shelves of vinyl and bought my first ever single there: 'Cum on Feel the Noize' by Slade, one of the best bands of the seventies. Noddy Holder's voice was easily the most recognisable in pop music, and still, today, if I hear it, I have to stop what I'm doing and listen. In my youth, supermarkets had yet to take the lion's share of grocery shopping. People used butchers for meats, greengrocers for fresh fruit and vegetables, and cheese, eggs, and cured meats could be found in a range of emporiums.

Mr Rowberry was Mam's butcher of choice. Much gossiping would be done by the Romany women who shopped at his establishment, and they regularly met outside on Union Street and in the shop between the hours of nine and midday. The floor was covered in a fine layer of sawdust, and cuts of meat were displayed under a glass counter; the choices were plentiful and always of excellent quality. Mam and the other Romany women who frequented his premises were valued, and Mr Rowberry often saved them the best joints and cuts of meats, giving rise to much resentment from some of the gorja customers. He was an avuncular, charming man who always had a kind word and was never too busy to stop and pass the time of day.

When I think of my early teenage years, they seem like halcyon days. Summers full of the heady aroma of flowers in bloom or winters with snow so deep that you could walk upon a hedge thinking it was the road. It isn't quite the whole picture, though. The seventies was a time of high unemployment with many strikes and rolling power cuts. None of this mattered to me as long as I had music to listen to. I loved bands such as Slade, as mentioned earlier, and Mud and The Sweet. Still, my personal favourite was considered to be less trendy: The New Seekers. They were a harmony group who, between 1970 and 1974, had massive success across the globe; with hits like 'Circles', 'I'd like to teach the world to sing' and 'Beg Steal or Borrow', they were always on my playlist. It was whilst playing their latest hit, 'You won't find another fool like me' in January 1974, that Dad came home early from work and announced that he and a fellow worker had been made redundant.

I knew this was something that could impact all our lives, but I probably didn't comprehend the full ramifications of what it meant. We were lucky, in that we didn't really want for anything. We always had enough food and decent clothing, and Dad kept a sizeable, well-tended garden where he enjoyed growing various seasonal vegetables. He had worked for the Barnes family on their farm in Monkhide, Herefordshire, for more than twelve years, along with several of his brothers and sisters who also stopped there, in fact, staying there for the remainder of their lives.

Farming was becoming increasingly mechanised, which meant that many labourers were no longer required to keep the farms going. Older men like me Dad, who was then in his early sixties, were often first in the line of fire for redundancy. One of Dad's younger brothers, Uncle Aldy, stopped with us and was employed at Claston Farm in Dormington, Herefordshire. Uncle Aldy was a lovely man whose heart was broken when Mam's sister Aunt Tilly married Johnny Jones. No other woman came close to gaining Aldy's affection, and he remained single for the rest of his life. He had been in the army during the Second World War. However, he had spent much of the war locked up for poggering a senior officer who he had overheard making derogatory remarks about Gypsies.

When Uncle Aldy returned home that evening, he, Dad, and Mam sat around the campfire talking about Dad's predicament. I carried on spinning records, only half listening, until I heard Dad say that there had been no warning of redundancy and they had not been offered any severance pay. This made me look up sharply and say, "They can't do that." All went quiet momentarily, and then Dad asked what I meant. I explained that I had learned about employment law at school a few months earlier and that, when people were made redundant, they were due to receive severance pay from their employer as long as they had been employed for over a year or had a contract.

A discussion followed about the chances of Dad winning if he took the farmer, who had also been a magistrate, to a tribunal. Dad and Mam thought there was little chance of success and worried about the cost of a solicitor against what they might win, but at one point, Uncle Aldy said that Dad could represent himself. Even though Dad had taught himself to read and write, his handwriting and spelling were poor. I piped up that I could fill in all the forms and go with him to court. Uncle Aldy winked at me and, looking at Dad, said, "What have you got to lose?"

The following Saturday, I went to the library in Hereford and took copious notes while reading and re-reading The Redundancy Payments Act 1965. I felt sure that Dad had a case for wrongful dismissal. Several months later, the case was heard at the magistrate's court in the Shirehall in Hereford. At the age of thirteen, I took a day off school and accompanied Dad to court to represent him in the case.

The farmer looked annoyed to be in the courtroom, and when the magistrate asked, "Is there anything you would like to say, Mr Smith?" Dad stood up and said, "My son will speak for me, sir." The magistrate and the farmer looked shocked as I rose to my feet, wearing my school uniform, and began reading the salient notes I had taken with me. I noticed that the magistrate and farmer, who was in the witness box, kept glancing at each other.

When I had finished, the farmer tried to imply that Dad was not capable of completing the workload he expected. This infuriated and enraged me inwardly, but on the outside, I remained as impassive as I could, given the circumstances, and questioned the farmer as to whether he had issued my father with any verbal or written warnings. He reluctantly admitted that he hadn't. The magistrate gave the farmer a long, knowing look, then said quickly that he was adjourning the case for seven days and hoped the parties could come to some resolution in that time.

As we left the court, Dad put his hand on my shoulder and said, "Thank you, my boy."

I replied, "I think we might have rattled them, Dad."

Dad said thoughtfully, "Yes, I think so."

That evening, Uncle Herbert, another of Dad's brothers, arrived at our tan. He exclaimed that whatever had happened in the court hearing had angered the farmer immensely and that he had been in a foul mood all afternoon and was spotted, red-faced, kicking buckets around the farmyard. Several days later, Dad received an offer of settlement through the post of quite a considerable sum for the time. Enough indeed that he didn't need to worry about getting another job in a hurry; in fact, he never went back to full-time employment, instead choosing seasonal work when he wanted and hawking when he fancied it until he retired. My father enjoyed freedom from the grind of labouring in his later years that many others had no option but to endure.

Chapter Seven

Karmic Irony

Our heritage and history come from India, and most of my bloodlines originated in the foothills of the Himalayas. However, not all of my mother's family are as complicated and diverse. As a child, I loved to sit and listen when my parents talked about 'the olden days'. My maternal great-grandfather was not a Gypsy or Traveller: Harry Carling, an Irishman from Limerick, in the county of the same name in Southwest Ireland, came from a well-to-do family. Mam said he left the land of his birth in his mid-twenties after a violent, drunken altercation with another man resulted in the man's death. His family, who owned a market garden business, helped him escape capture by stowing him away in a barrel on a boat bound for north Wales and bribed the captain to ensure Harry reached his destination. After landing, he then travelled to Cardiff before arriving in the Pontypool area. There, he met and fell in love with eighteen-year-old Sabrina Smith, a strikingly beautiful, raven-haired, Welsh Romany Gypsy.

After they married, Harry took Sabrina's surname, almost certainly to avoid detection for his wrongdoing. He was lean, dark, and swarthy and grew a full, unruly beard that obscured his handsome features yet complimented his quiet, secretive personality. Harry's crime was rumoured to have been motivated by jealousy over a woman. It is said that he was courting and hoping to marry a pretty girl whom he had agreed to meet at a local dance. Upon his arrival, he saw his sweetheart romantically kissing another man. Harry was enraged and humiliated, and a fight ensued with the rival suitor, culminating in Harry throwing his adversary down some concrete steps, unintentionally breaking his neck.

Harry himself, in what was reported as his soft, deep, Irish brogue, chose not to elaborate, so the whole truth is unknown. Whatever the speculation, he never returned to Ireland. Harry and Sabrina travelled around Wales with their oldest children, but they did not linger in one place for too long, eventually arriving in the Leominster area of Herefordshire, where they completed their family. Sabrina and Harry had seven children, of which Jeremiah, my grandfather, was one. His siblings were Thomas, Brookie, Timothy, Joeb, Amos, and the only girl, Caroline, known as Cassie.

Harry's family was well off, and they regularly sent him money. Consequently, he and Sabrina could always afford high-quality wagons and horses. Often, to confuse the pursuers who were still looking to bring him to justice, Harry would go by the name John Smith, along with various other pseudonyms. Harry died between 1910 and 1920; the exact year is unknown to me. Family lore has it that he was riding home after a night's drinking at a local inn when (it is presumed) he fell from his horse and, in what could be considered karmic irony, broke his neck. I don't think it can be ruled out that his pursuers, male members of the family of the man he had killed, had caught up with him and dished out their own form of retribution, but there is no evidence for this.

Harry Carling is buried in an unmarked plot in a small village churchyard near Leominster. Sabrina refused to have a headstone on the grave, and his resting place has no marker, because the day after the funeral, when Sabrina returned, she removed the metal burial plaque saying, "Now they will never find you, and you can finally sleep easy".

Mam said that she would often accompany her father when he visited his mother in her later years following Harry's death. Sabrina, by this time, had lost her eyesight and most of her good looks due to years of hard work and grief after losing the love of her life. Mam reported that, even after all she had endured, Sabrina still retained her inner glow, enjoyed smoking her clay pipe, and was one of the kindest people she had ever known, unlike Mam's maternal grandmother, whom she described as 'the old witch'.

Mam's mother, Lavinia, died of tuberculosis in her early thirties after birthing six children, leaving my granddad bereft. Following Lavinia's passing, her mother (the old witch) attempted to have all six children taken into care, saying she didn't believe that Jeremiah could successfully look after them alone whilst travelling on the road. To keep his family together, a grieving Jeremiah took employment on a hop farm near Burley Gate, called Whittick Manor, at that time. He knew the farmer, having previously stopped on a piece of land that the farmer-owned called 'Chitty Hom' when hop or fruit picking. It was during this period that Jeremiah learned that one of his brothers had been killed.

Granddad's brother Amos was out hare coursing and poaching with a couple of other Romany men, near Staunton-on-Wye in West Herefordshire. They had made their tan, with their wagons and horses, a couple of miles away at Bredwardine and had walked to Staunton, not wanting to be seen breaking the law near to their stopping place. They were on their way back to the tan, carrying what would have been their evening meals, when they were confronted by a gamekeeper who was bearing a shotgun. The keeper challenged them, and demanded they relinquish the rabbits that Amos's Lurcher dog had killed. The two men with Amos threw their rabbits to the ground, before running away as fast as their legs could carry them. Amos, however, known for being handy with his fists and having a hot temper to match, refused to do so and stood his ground. After a verbal argument, the fracas turned physical, and Amos and the gamekeeper began to brawl. During the fight Amos's Lurcher, in an attempt to protect him, became entangled between the two men causing Amos to trip and fall to the ground. The gun was discharged, and Amos was shot in his side.

This may or may not have been deliberate, and the keeper testified afterwards that it was an accident. Amos, though severely injured, managed to get to his feet and attempted to run back to his tan. On the way, though, probably through loss of blood, he collapsed, and close to his demise, crawled inside a hay barn. He was later discovered, having bled to death, with his dog sat faithfully by his side.

Mam and her siblings were thereafter brought up by my grandfather in a black and white timbered farm cottage, with leaded windows. Many gorjas believe, wrongly, that to be considered a Gypsy or Traveller you have to constantly travel. This implies that our ethnicity is based on how we live, rather than our bloodlines. Even today, government ministers and certain aspects of the press in this country perpetuate this misconception. The truth is not as clear cut: some Gypsies travel, on a full or part-time basis, others do not. Those that are settled don't stop being Gypsies and Travellers. Some members of my family have never travelled on the road in caravans, others have rarely stopped. Whether we travel or not is not what defines us. We are defined instead by our culture, heritage, and history.

Persecution of Travellers has always been prevalent in this country and across Europe. During the Second World War, it's estimated that between two and five hundred thousand Gypsies were exterminated by the Nazis in concentration camps. No one knows the true number as nobody bothered to count. We simply didn't matter, and still don't in the eyes of many people. Consequently, Gypsies and Travellers have often led a somewhat secretive existence. The census in 2021 recorded 71,400 Gypsies and Travellers in England and Wales. Every Traveller NGO (Non-Government Organisation) is aware, that this figure is a vast under representation. Many Travellers still deny their heritage to gorjas, and officials, out of fear of persecution and prejudice. The true number of Gypsies and Travellers currently in Britain could easily be up to one million people.

As Mam and her brothers and sisters grew up, they all married and went back on the road. As did granddad Jeremiah before meeting his second wife, Granny Rose, who was a widow with four children: Jimmy, Fezzy, Jobey, and Plezente, known as 'Baby'. Rose was a formidable, strong-minded woman who didn't suffer fools gladly. She also believed strongly in the unseen world, and was highly intuitive, often making predictions that were uncannily accurate. Mam and Rose got along well, Mam realising that Rose loved my grandfather very much. Together, Rose and Jeremiah had five children, meaning that Mam now had five full-blood brothers and sisters, as well as four step siblings, and five half brothers and sisters. Mam always referred to any of the children as brother or sister, not differentiating outwardly between their parental differences.

Rose and my grandfather moved into a black and white cottage, next to the churchyard in Weston Beggard, Herefordshire, where they reared their five children, Mary, Amelia, Tommy, Sybil, and Nelson. Rose adored and cared for my grandfather until his death from cancer, in March 1963. Mam and Dad went to see Jeremiah at his home in Church House Cottage on what would be his final day. Shortly before he breathed his last breath, my grandfather took my mother's hand in his and kissed her cheek. He then looked at his daughter and said, "It's going to be a very long dark toratii, my wench." The word 'toratii' means night or this evening in Romanes. These were the last words my mother ever heard her father speak to her; and she never forgot them.

In her later years, Granny Rose and her youngest son, Nelson, often stopped with us in one of the sheds at hop picking time. She would always ensure that she brought sweets home when she went shopping, and I was hardly ever without Sherbet Dabs or chocolate when she returned.

Chapter Eight
The Cool Gang

At primary school, the only bullying I experienced from another pupil occurred when I was six in 1967, just after my brother had purchased his blue Ford Transit truck. He dropped me off outside Yarkhill School and stood observing me as I walked into the playground. My brother, Len, named after my father, was twenty years old at the time, and there are fourteen years between us. Len was good-looking and popular with the girls; he modelled himself on Paul McCartney and liked to wear stylish suits and shoes. This morning, though, he was wearing his overalls and a woollen hat. As he watched me safely into the yard, an older, much larger boy came over to me and insisted that I fight him. As the boy began to push and shove me, I suddenly heard my brother's voice ring out, "Oi!" he shouted, "If you touch him again, I'll kick your arse, and when you get home tell your father that I'll kick his arse too". The boy immediately changed tack, insisting that he was 'just playing'. Len scowled at him, and the boy ran into the schoolhouse. I had no more trouble with bullies at primary school after that. However, the same blue Ford Transit truck would be the cause of a period of sustained, nasty bullying at my subsequent education establishment.

In 1972, I graduated from primary school to secondary school. My brother, Len, had attended Canon Frome School some years earlier and was able to give me a heads up about what to expect, although it appeared that he had spent much of his time there working in the large walled-in garden rather than in lessons. Most of the country was on strike, including the miners and dockers. The miner's strike had been declared a national emergency. Anti-British riots were taking place all across Ireland, mainly because the British Army had shot thirteen unarmed nationalist civil rights marchers in Derry, Northern Ireland. Several British businesses had been burned to the ground, along with the British Embassy. Civil unrest was in the air.

This was not what worried me, though. The move to a new school occupied my thoughts a lot. I'm sure many gorja children felt apprehensive also, but it was a challenging time for Gypsy and Traveller kids. At my second junior school, bullying was firmly discouraged, and most of us Romany children experienced little or no direct prejudice because of our ethnicity. This changed dramatically when we moved to 'big' school.

Mam and Dad were keen that I should not be treated differently because of my ethnicity. They felt it was vital that I had a proper school uniform, even though it could only be purchased from an expensive outfitter's in Ledbury. The blazers for Canon Frome were dark blue with sky-blue edging. The top left pocket had an unusual image of a Griffin holding a man's hand dripping with blood sewn onto it. I had done well in education at my first two schools and was considered by my teachers to be academically bright. So, I was stunned when, on the first day, which for some reason was a Wednesday, my cousin, Michael, and I were placed in the 'slow learners' class, along with several other Romanies and a number of gorja children. Upon returning home that evening, I declared that I wouldn't be going again. Mam and Dad looked at each other knowingly, and Mam asked me why. When I told her what had happened and that I'd spent most of the day digging in the garden, a look of anger and defiance came upon her, and she told me not to worry about it; she would sort it out.

Mr Zeuner, the science teacher at Canon Frome, lived just up the road from our tan in a large house that had once been a rectory. He was an interesting man; his dream was to replicate Hannibal's expedition across the Alps using elephants, and he spent much of his time raising funds for this. The following day, whilst walking past his house to get to the hop yards she was working in, Mam called in to see the teacher and ask why my cousin and I had been placed in the 'slow' class, considering our success at our previous school. Mr Zeuner said he had no idea and admitted that it seemed strange. He suggested that Mam speak directly with the headmaster, Mr Godfrey, taking my previous school reports with her.

The following day, during lunchtime, Mam was driven to the school by my brother. She insisted on seeing Mr Godfrey and said she would wait until he was free. To this day, I don't know what was said in the meeting, only that when Michael and I returned to school the following week, we were intercepted by a teacher straight after assembly, who told us that a mistake had been made and that we were to join the regular students in their classes. Most of the other Romany kids stayed in the 'slow' class, not because they were 'slow', but because some had received little schooling before attending secondary school, usually due to the fact that they had been on the road, and had only recently settled in one place long enough to make it worthwhile going.

Mr Zeuner kept an eye on me and my progress for the rest of the year, ensuring that he was always available should I need to speak with him. I made friends easily, but my major concern was whether to tell them about my ethnicity. My cousin Michael was tall, strong, and a good fighter, so the gorja kids mainly left him to his own devices. I wasn't a good fighter and depended on my personality and wits to get through. Sometimes this worked, sometimes it did not, but mostly, my time at Canon Frome was marred by the anxiety of my ethnicity being discovered. Many of the children came from poor backgrounds and often us Gypsies were better dressed and had more money than them. This in itself could cause issues with jealousy.

I wanted to be in the cool gang, but to do this; I believed that I needed to learn to smoke. At the age of thirteen, I chored (stole) a couple of cigarettes from Mam's pack one Saturday afternoon and found a quiet spot to light up. Mam smoked Park Drive cigarettes that were strong and didn't even have a filter on. I took a long drag, inhaled, and promptly passed out. You would think that this deterred me from the addictive weed, but no. I woke up feeling dizzy with my head spinning, but also determined to continue; I soon became an expert smoker. Choring from Mam was not on though, which I knew.

The cool kids all smoked. Canon Frome School was a large converted country house, which was pretty much a mansion as far as I was concerned. The extensive grounds included large playing fields, an outdoor swimming pool, hard tennis courts, and even a lake (with a tree-covered island in the middle) where we went canoeing. Behind the island was the perfect spot in which to hide from the gaze of teachers, the trees and vegetation shielding us from the staff's sight while we sat in our canoe's sharing fags and smoking.

Due to its location in the heart of the countryside, pretty much all of the pupils were bussed into Canon Frome. I had to walk half a mile to catch the school bus that was driven by a woman called Mrs Whitehead, who had no truck with any trouble on her vehicle and was not to be messed with. The journey took us through Monkhide, which had a shop at the end of the village. Several kids, including me, would jump off the bus outside the shop, and while it was turning around at the end of the road, we would rush into the shop ostensibly to buy sweets but, in reality, to purchase cigarettes. Black Cat and Number Six were the most popular brands and our favourites at that time.

This went on for several months until, one Sunday, my brother and Dad came home from their lunchtime drink at the Newtown pub, which overlooked the crossroads at the edge of the village. Len waited until we were all sat down enjoying our roast dinner before disclosing, with a tone of mischief in his voice, that he had been told at the pub about me and other kids buying fags at Monkhide shop on the way to school. My jaw dropped open with my forkful of food in mid-air, halfway on its journey to my mouth. I couldn't believe he was telling on me!

My brother had a satisfied grin on his face as Mam and Dad started on at me about smoking. Dad had given up several years earlier and was particularly vehement in his denouncement. Mam gave my brother a stern look, saying, "You just had to bring this up at dinner time, didn't you?" She knew full well that Dad would soon be saying that she should quit also. None of this made me give up smoking, though; so strong was the youthful need to appear 'cool' and then, inevitably, the addiction to nicotine that it would be a significant health scare forty years later that finally made me stop. I still miss it.

I enjoyed the learning aspect of going to school but was constantly worried that my 'friends' would discover my ethnicity and judge me harshly for it, as they did to other Gypsies who attended. My cousin, Shirley, who was slightly older than me, was once stabbed in the leg with a lead pencil by another girl simply for the 'crime' of being Romany. She didn't even bother to report the assault, knowing that it was unlikely that anything would be done. Name-calling, using what would now be considered racist terms, was common and frequent. The kids who behaved in this manner did so with impunity. Unlike primary school, in secondary, these issues were pretty much ignored by the teachers unless severe violence was used. If this was the case, it was inevitably the Gypsy children who were punished, sometimes with canings, but more often with suspensions or even expulsion. Unfortunately, little has changed, even today. Gypsies and Travellers are often asked to leave a school when it is they who are the victims of racist attacks. In many educational establishments, it's the preferred way of dealing with the matter of racism towards Gypsy and Traveller children. Often, it's not even recognised as bigotry at all, usually being seen as a 'white on white' issue and, therefore, not racist.

There have been many cases in recent years. One Romany Gypsy child was set on and severely injured by a large group of boys. This happened in a playground whilst teachers looked on and chose not to intervene. None of the perpetrators were suspended or expelled, but the Romany child was asked to leave, his parents being told by the head teacher that their boys' safety could not be guaranteed and he would be better off being home-schooled by his parents. He later spoke about his experience on a national television programme after winning the Diana Award for his work on Gypsy and Traveller awareness, but it's made little difference to most children's struggles. My own experience of racism and prejudice during my school years in the 1970s was one of constant anguish. I tried not to show my feelings to my parents, as I did not want them to worry about me. It was also mixed with a sense of shame, and it was pernicious in its effects on my mental health. Anxiety was a perpetual factor that I had to learn to deal with. It was wearying and hugely affected my enjoyment of my secondary school years.

One of the major school bullies at Canon Frome appeared halfway through a term when I was fourteen. He lived in Tarrington and caught the same school bus as me. It transpired that he had already been expelled from one school for bad behaviour. Even now, I cannot bring myself to write this boy's name; the thought of him still fills me with anger and loathing. I had to walk half a mile from our tan to catch the bus to school and the same distance home on the return journey. The weather on the day in question was appalling. It had rained heavily the entire day, and I was not looking forward to the walk home from the bus stop, so I was pleased when I saw my brother's blue transit truck waiting for me. As the bus slowed, I heard the bully shout from the back seat, "That's a gypo's truck". I ignored this as best I could and got off the bus. The pleasure of my brother giving me a lift home was now coupled with anxiety about how this would play out at school the next day. I said nothing to Len about how I was feeling, though, as I was embarrassed to show my concern about what might happen.

As we disembarked inside the school gates the next day, the boy sidled up to me and whispered into my ear, "All right, gypo?" I had a sinking feeling in my stomach but carried on walking, attempting to brush off what he had said. The boy sneered at me and laughed in a way that made me think this was just the start and that there would be plenty more to come. I was right.

Over the next few weeks and months, the bullying from this boy and two of his cohorts heightened in intensity. It was insidious in its nature, designed to make me nervous and exist in a state of perpetual angst. At no point did it occur to me to report what was happening to any of the teaching staff, even our neighbour, Mr Zeuner. Similarly, I felt unable to tell my parents or brother. The shame the bullying engendered was palpable, and it affected me in ways that nearly fifty years later I am still coming to terms with.

As well as the racist name-calling, the bullies upped the ante, cornering me in toilets or empty classrooms and pushing and shoving me around. This increased in severity to ripping lumps of hair off my head or trying to force me to eat inedible items, like leaves, dirt, and, once, dog excrement. They did this whilst taunting me by saying, "Go on, gypo, eat it; you eat hedgehogs, don't ya?" This was said in the form of a statement rather than a question that could be disputed. My cousin Michael, who, due to his stature and fighting prowess, had no issues with anyone daring to bully him, would give me a pitying, withering look if he saw what was happening that said, 'For God's sake, stand up for yourself; it's shameful to let them treat you like that'. I was so cowed and intimidated by this time, though, that I could not imagine standing up to these dangerous, Machiavellian, and conniving kids.

It was common knowledge within the school that my main bully's father had been in and out of prison several times for violent crimes. In retrospect, this might go some way to explaining my tormentor's behaviour. But the day it all came to a head, I looked into his small, vindictive eyes and knew that something deep in his soul was rotten. I was isolated by my harassers in the Geography room. The bane of my life came over to me in his nasty and intimidating way. At the same time, his disciples watched with gleeful expectation, occasionally glancing at the door to ensure they wouldn't be disturbed. He began in his usual way by pinching and using a low voice to racially abuse me. It was now more than an issue of race, though; it had become about breaking me mentally, as well as physically.

With the onlookers now excitedly hopping from foot to foot with presumptive anticipation, the bully grabbed the collar of my blazer, pulling me closer before saying; "My dad hates gypo's. He says we're gonna burn your stinking caravan to the ground, with you and your knacker family inside." The menace in his voice led me immediately to realise that this was not an idle threat. Something inside me snapped: for a brief moment, I was no longer myself. I could hear the blood rushing in my ears and feel my heart hammering in my chest. I took a step back, clenched my right fist, and hit him as hard as I could under his left eye. Looking surprised and shocked, he stumbled slightly, and it was then that I took the opportunity to kick his legs out from under him. He crashed to the floor, cracking his head loudly on a wooden chair as he descended.

Everything in the room stilled for a moment. The two disciples started moving towards me when Michael suddenly appeared in the doorway, out of what seemed nowhere. He grabbed the throat of the nearest boy to him, warning, "Say anything, and there will be worse for both of you." He released his grip and the disciples slunk from the room.

I looked down to see blood dripping from my tyrant's head, yet he still looked up at me with murderous intent in his piggy eyes. The thought crossed my mind that he would almost certainly kill me when he stood up. I was, I think, in shock at my behaviour. I really couldn't believe what I had done. As he began to rise inexorably to his feet, my cousin strode over, placed his hand on the bully's forehead, and pushed him back to the floor, saying, "Stay down fucker, cos' he's not on his own now." Michael glared menacingly at my intimidator before looking at me with what appeared to be a newfound respect and said simply, "Let's go."

Although the bullying didn't stop completely, I had little trouble with the main culprit after that incident. Pupils' abusing each other verbally is part of school life and takes many forms, not just racial. It is when the harassment is sustained over a long period that it does the most damage. Any child who is considered different can experience this. Still, it's far more common for Gypsies and Travellers, and for us, it is generally not treated with the seriousness it deserves – or not recognised at all.

Chapter Nine
Japes and Mistakes

Although Dad taught himself to read and write, he did so at a reasonably low level. He could read his own name and address and write them using mainly capital letters, but his understanding of more complex words was poor. He often needed to ask me what a word meant or how it was pronounced. Mam never learned to read or write and had no official schooling at all. Most of the time, this did not bother her; she would recognise brand names whilst shopping by their colour and design, but this could occasionally bring about mistakes that were both unintentionally amusing and potentially dangerous. Mam always splashed out food-wise on weekends. Choice cuts of steak, or large pieces of cod, on Saturdays, and lamb, beef, or pork joints for Sunday lunch. Chicken was usually a midweek meal for us. Most of our meals were plain and simple food cooked from scratch. We didn't really do ready meals, as Mam often didn't understand what exactly it was that the packaging contained.

One Saturday evening Mam was in the shed, frying steak to go with roast potatoes and green beans. As she did so, she absentmindedly placed what she thought was a new container of Saxa salt on the table. I was amusing myself with the latest Beano, or Whizzer and Chips comic, and Dad was using a bowl of water outside to wash his hands and face. Mam called us both inside to eat the now-ready food that she was dishing up. Dad went inside first, sat at the table, sprinkled some 'salt' on his food and began eating heartily. It took me a couple of minutes to finish reading the story I was engaged with, and Mam had to call me for a second time.

Stuffing the comic into my jeans pocket, I quickly entered the shed, sat at the table, and reached for the 'salt'. "What's the Ajax doing on the table?" I asked, picking it up.

Mam replied, "No, that's salt."

"It's not," I said. "It's definitely Ajax."

Dad looked up and paused, having already eaten half of his meal. "What's that?" he asked.

"It's Ajax, Dad," I replied, "Cleaning powder; it says here that it kills all known germs."

The colour quickly drained out of my mother's face as Dad began spitting steak remnants out of his mouth onto his plate. "Oh God, Betty", he spluttered, "You've poisoned me."

"I thought it was salt," said Mam worriedly. "It looks like salt." To be fair, the Saxa and Ajax containers did look remarkably similar, and I could understand how Mam had made a mistake. I began to laugh uncontrollably while Dad was busy swilling his mouth out with milk Mam had handed him, with an apologetic look on her face. Luckily, Dad had no lasting effects from Mam's error, but he did double-check what he was adding to his meal afterwards.

For a boy growing up in the 1970s, owning a Raleigh Chopper bike was de rigueur. Mine was bright orange, and whilst the seat was uncomfortable and the frame quite heavy, it was also completely cool. I tried to keep my prize in mint condition. Washing, polishing, and oiling it regularly. I went everywhere on my bike and loved the freedom it gave me. It was a bugger to ride wearing flares though, and these had to be wrapped around the ankles, and tucked inside socks, to avoid getting caught in the bike chain, somewhat spoiling the trendy image.

Fashion was important: we wore flowery shirts with long pointed or rounded collars, striped tank tops, denim jackets, and jeans that had to be Levi or Wrangler to be considered on trend, and of course, teardrop-shaped sunglasses that preferably had to be 'Reactolite'. This was the look that many boys aspired to, unless they were skinheads, which I definitely wasn't. My hair was so long at one point that I was regularly mistaken for a girl from behind. Strangely, most school teachers tolerated this, and several younger teachers at Canon Frome wore their hair long, too. Some didn't, though, and Bill Close, the deputy head, who was mostly bald and we nicknamed 'Badger', would often admonish those of us with hair longer than our collars, saying, "Get a haircut, boy." We mainly ignored this 'advice'. The deputy head took great delight in confiscating any cigarettes he found us with. He would then leave the staff room door open at break times, where he could be observed puffing away on *our* fags, with a satisfied, almost smirking look on his face.

I hated woodwork. I was inept and, looking back, lazy when it came to this lesson. I didn't want to do it and barely tried. It took me three years to make a stool with a raffia seat. Mr Close refused to let me move on to another project until I'd finished it. I resolved to take as long as possible and spent most of the class time talking to other students, mucking about, or staring through the windows, wishing that time would speed up and bring the boredom to an end. At the beginning of the 4th year, I could choose which lessons I concentrated on, with a few mandatory exceptions, like English, Mathematics, and P.E. English was the lesson I cherished most, and it was the subject I was best at. I loved reading and still do. Books were, and still are, an escape to another world. One of the set books that we had to study for our exams was 'Lord of the Flies' by William Golding. The book explored how quickly humans, in this case, children, could return to savagery given the right circumstances.

I have always had the ability to read and experience the emotions of others. I describe myself as an empath. Some people refer to this ability as a gift, but I don't because I know how distressing and exhausting it can be. I find it intensely uncomfortable to be around people who are exuding negative emotions, often when they don't even realise how they are feeling themselves. Some people put on a veneer of pleasantness, but I can always tell how they feel underneath the pretence. Over the years, I have had to learn how to protect myself from the destructive emotions of others. I imagine a white light surrounding me, like the 'Ready Brek' cereal glow, as seen on television adverts in my childhood.

Usually, this works, but exceptionally powerful emotions can break through my defences, like a dirty, industrial, swollen river releasing its floodwater and rushing down a nearby street, creeping under the front doors of the occupants who live there, letting the feelings enter my mind, polluting my equilibrium. If it becomes detrimental to my mental or physical health, my only recourse is to put distance between myself and the person. There have been a few occasions where I have had to call time on relationships permanently when I have found them too distressing or unpleasant to be around.

I wasn't keen on P.E. (Physical Education), and cross-country running was an activity I particularly reviled. Due to Canon Frome School being deep in the Herefordshire countryside, it really was 'across country'. The first part of the course was to run the length of the half-mile private road that led to the school. We had to go as far as the iron and pillared gates, adorned on top with stone statues of Griffins, and then double back, halfway to the school, before turning left through a farm gate into the surrounding fields. We then ran because, at this point, we were still observable by the P.E. master, using his binoculars, down a farm track that led across a bridge to another field on the opposite side of the river.

By this time, I and a few other boys were exhausted and, knowing we could no longer be seen, had decelerated to a slow trot and, in some boy's cases, including mine, a walk. It was at this stage that the fags were shared out and lit up. The real runners were off in the distance, trying their best to outdo each other. My friends and I cared little about this, content to do a mixture of strolling and jogging along, in no real hurry to return to the abhorred showers. I'm unsure of exactly how long the course was, probably four or five miles at least; whatever the length, it seemed too long for us.

To get back across the river, we had to traverse a large, thick log with iron railings on either side of it that spanned the width of the river. I've always had a bit of a phobia about crossing bridges and never looked forward to that part of the run. I'm sure health and safety would not allow it these days, but in the 1970s no such concerns were apparent. The log bridge ushered us to a shaded tree-lined path that led to the outdoor swimming pool in what was known as the stable block. The rest of the slow contingent and I usually came last or near to it in the run, none of us caring which of us actually crossed the finish line in the final position. Except for on this occasion; halfway down the lane that led from the log bridge to the swimming pool we saw a derelict, ivy-clad stone chalet on the riverbank. During one run, we noticed that a wild bee's nest was halfway up the wall facing the path.

Three of us hatched a plan during the intervening week. We thought it would be a bit of a jape to throw rocks at the bee's nest and see what happened when the runners came down the path. To make the plan work, we had to compete in the cross-country run. Coming in last, as usual, would not be enough to ensure the success of the machination. On the day in question, we ran as fast as we could to get in front of as many pupils as possible. The class was double its usual size, as the girls were competing too on this occasion. The elite runners were well out in front, and even though we were doing our best, there was no hope of catching them. We were in the middle of the pack and had to wait until there was a convenient break in the group before enacting our plan.

Unobserved, we stopped near the chalet and waited for our moment. We grabbed a few bricks and stones of a reasonable size and threw them at the hole halfway up the wall, where the industrious bees could be seen entering and exiting their hive. Most missed their mark, but a couple didn't. The bees swarmed out of the hole and filled the air with angry buzzing. We legged it down the path to a safe distance and then hid and watched as a number of pupils came around the corner, running straight into the enraged swarm. Within a few moments, we knew we had made a big mistake. Boys and girls, wearing shorts and tee shirts, began to scream and frantically bat the bees away with their hands. Our 'jape' had turned into a scene from a horror movie. We watched, aghast, as one girl with long auburn ringleted hair raced past us, with bees covering her Bonnie Langford-style locks. We, too, were now surrounded by buzzing, highly irritated insects and joined the pupils running as fast as they could away from the scene. As we reached the pool, we witnessed the frenzied spectacle of kids jumping into the water to rid themselves of the agitated wild bees. By this time, we were also being stung on our arms and legs.

As things began to calm down a little and the bees retreated into their hive, we looked at each other and knew, without saying it aloud, that we could never admit to what we had done. We feared that the punishment for this transgression would, at the very least, be a caning by the headmaster and possibly expulsion. Many kids were stung, although thankfully, none seriously. The girl with the ringlets was actually only stung once. Unfortunately, it was in the spot above her nose and between her eyebrows. She was left with two swollen black eyes that lasted a fortnight. I felt ashamed of what we had done every time I looked at her. That shame and guilt, coupled with the contrary emotion that makes some people laugh inappropriately at funerals, is still with me to this day.

Chapter Ten
Signs and Portents

My mother believed that a pill was always available to cure any ailment. Her faith in this astounded me. What she was really looking for was a medication that could take away the pain of the loss that she felt. Loss of loved ones, loss of youth, and a loss of hope affected her happiness. Mam's depression expressed itself in a variety of imaginary medical maladies. Her hypochondria tormented her stability and had detrimental effects on those of us around her, especially me. I didn't just observe her psychological pain; I experienced it as only someone with empathic abilities can. However, the reverse scenario was also true. When my mother was on good form, I experienced a sense of lightness of being that expanded my soul and stirred my heart with an almost overwhelming love for life. I liked to spend these times in the open countryside, encompassed by nature.

Opposite Yarkhill church, there is a small green field with a cow shed on one side. At the edge of the field is a moat surrounding a rectangular parcel of land on which a house with a water mill once stood. I spent hours there, watching the ducks and moorhens paddling around on the water and listening to the throaty call and reply coos of the wood pigeons. All manner of wildlife and insects visited this area. I had no idea, at the time, that the site was one of a number in the Herefordshire countryside that was of national importance. A notice there now informs visitors that the site was inhabited during Roman times and long after.

To get onto the island, two strands of thick wire were strung between posts spaced four feet apart on either side of the moat. I had to hold onto the top wire whilst carefully taking sliding steps on the lower one. The cables, even though tightly strung, would wobble crazily as I got near the centre, which added to the thrill without there being any real danger. If I did fall into the water below, as long as I landed on my feet, then only my shoes and trousers would get wet; the moat was relatively shallow, especially during the summer months, and covered with various water-based plants.

I liked to sit on the island, surrounded by the greenery, watching insects such as brilliantly iridescent dragonflies and green beetles that looked like leaves, with ladybugs landing on my arms and legs before they lifted off in flight like helicopters. Common blue, Tortoiseshell, Red Admiral, and Peacock butterflies were abundant, and if I was really lucky, I would see a Great Crested Newt, that are a rarity these days, with only a few breeding grounds left in the country.

Oftentimes, I would take the latest 'Secret Seven' paperback by Enid Blyton with me, or perhaps 'The Silver Sword' by Ian Serraillierr or any book by Alan Garner that I could get my hands on. Alan Garner was my favourite author. I marvelled at the way he could take a normal situation and turn it into something magical, as he did with his fantasy novel 'Elidor'. I was often alone, yet rarely felt lonely. My imagination could fill my mind with exciting possibilities, and I always had the ever-present feeling that the man in blue was nearby, watching over me. We had conversations that took place in my mind, and I sometimes learned of future events before they happened.

I occasionally told my parents about my intuitions but realised I had to be careful about how I did this. Every so often, Mam would give me a look of puzzlement mixed with concern if my portents were too exact. I found it was better to be a little vague or not to say anything at all. I was fascinated with the idea of telepathy and loved to watch television shows like 'The Champions', a 1960s TV series about secret agents with extra sensory powers. As I grew into a teenager, my own experiences with the unseen world became more vivid and regular in their occurrence.

My paternal grandmother, Granny Ada, died in hospital on the 24th of September 1974, at the age of 76. Granny passed ten years and eight days after Granddad Sam, who had died of cancer on the 16th day of the same month in 1964. Granny had been taken into Hereford General Hospital at three thirty in the afternoon the previous day. She died within twelve hours of meningitis. She had walked to Monkhide stores to get some food for my aunts and Uncle Herbert's tea, who was in the last days of the hop picking season; while in the shop, she began to feel unwell, with a severe headache. When my aunts, Louise and Mary, arrived home earlier than usual, they discovered my grandmother unconscious in the wooden hut where they lived. The large hut, unlike ours, had several windows and contained a black-lead stove and several fine pieces of furniture, including a four-poster bed. Louise and Mary accompanied Granny Ada to the hospital whilst Uncle Herbert came to our tan to tell us what had happened.

Mam and Dad had just arrived home from the hop yards, and after a quick wash and change of clothes, Mam insisted that Uncle Aldy drive her to the hospital. When she arrived, she found Louise and Mary in a highly distressed state. Neither could cope with the idea that they might lose their mother after the loss of their father ten years before. Uncle Aldy drove both of them home to gather their composure and await news of Granny's situation before returning to the hospital himself to be with his mother. As Granny's condition deteriorated, he also found it too intense and overpowering in emotion to stay on the ward with her, preferring to sit in the waiting room and prepare for the outcome. Mam, though, refused to leave Granny's side; she sat beside her, holding her hand, and whispered to her reassuringly to let her mother-in-law know she wasn't alone. Mam understood grief and death. She had already seen both of her parents pass over and had endured the tragedies of two of her brothers departing in difficult and unusual circumstances.

Granny Ada never regained consciousness. She passed between 3am and 4am in the morning. The hour when we believe the veil between life and death is at its thinnest. Hours before she died, Granny Ada visited me. My sister and her family were stopping with us at Yarkhill Farm at the time, as they had done for several years. My niece, Jenny, was only three years younger than me, and we always felt we were more like siblings than uncle and niece, even attending the same schools together.

Romany children are not shielded from the reality of death, as gorja kids often are. We attended funerals from a young age and were supported through the upsetting, byzantine emotions that grief brings. Many of my classmates at school could not believe that I was, at the age of thirteen, allowed to attend my grandmother's funeral. One girl was singularly shocked, as she hadn't been allowed to attend her own mother's funeral a few months earlier. In fact, it was a year before she even visited her mother's grave, and I know that she found that whole period of her life incredibly upsetting and confusing. She was not permitted to grieve and move on in a natural way. Romany children are usually very aware of the cycle of life and death and are deeply aware that all beginnings have an end.

Jenny and I were outside, sat on the grass, facing the road, with our backs against the gate that opened into Mr Dufty's orchard, where several of our horses were kept. The Dufty's had moved into the house just up the road and were friendly, pleasant people who always made time to stop and converse. Mam and Dad spent a lot of time with them, and they enjoyed learning about our culture and heritage. We were waiting for Mam to return with news of Granny's condition. It was around seven thirty, and the twilight had yet to move into the darkness of night. As we sat on the increasingly dewy grass, we watched the full harvest moon rise over the distant hills of Mordiford and listened to the abundant insects and the first hoots of the nearby owls.

The first indication I had that something unexpected was about to happen was a gurgling sound. It would be many years before I heard this sound again, but I know now that it was a death rattle. I then experienced a sensation that became all too familiar over the intervening years. I suddenly felt very emotional. This sensitiveness began at the top of my head and then poured, like a waterfall, into every part of my body, completely filling me up. I had no idea whether I would laugh or cry; both emotions felt oddly appropriate. It was then that I saw my grandmother standing in the middle of the road before me. She appeared completely real, yet I knew she could not be there. She smiled, waved, and blew me a kiss before turning and walking into the creeping darkness, slowly disappearing. I would later find out from my mother that she had been in a coma at the time of my seeing her and was in the process of passing over. Jenny, noticing that something was wrong, asked what the matter was. I replied that I had just seen Granny waving at us.

My niece, who was a little spooked, ran to my sister's trailer to gain reassurance. I stood, looking at the now empty road, a deep sadness washing over me as the realisation of what the visitation meant formed in my mind. Shortly after, Dad came out and called me inside; as I walked with him, I told him what I had seen. He nodded his head but said nothing. He waited up through the night until my mother returned, in the early hours of the following day, with the news that he already knew and was by then prepared for.

Signs and portents from the unseen world are not the only ones that come to Gypsy and Traveller people. My father was especially adept at picking up cues for what was to come for us. Successive British governments have been the precursor of signals for how our lives would be changed: traditional stopping places have systematically been closed off for our use; residential site provision has been underfunded and, in many cases, withdrawn; and changes in planning law have been exclusively changed. Many local authorities now only consider us to be Gypsies or Travellers, for planning purposes, if we are actually travelling. This suggests that governments and local authorities don't believe we are legitimate ethnic minorities. It's a bit like saying, to be considered Jewish; all Jewish people have to live in the state of Israel. It is unfair and discriminatory to deny the heritage of entire sections of society. Gypsies have a lower life expectancy than almost every other ethnic group in Britain. Lack of sites, either residential or transit, means that access to health care can be severely limited for those who wish to continue living in trailers.

Every day in Britain, reports in the press ascribe negative connotations onto the Gypsy and Traveller communities. Outside of the tabloids, the local press usually does the most damage to our reputations. Newspapers regularly allow comments on their stories about us online that are racist, discriminatory, and, in some cases, even incite murder. Threats of violence and offers to burn down our homes, with us inside them, are frequently allowed to stand on press websites. These comments would never be tolerated by any other ethnic group.

The judicial system is also an issue, with many judges and people in authority or positions of influence simply not accepting that what we regularly experience is racism because we are considered to be white. There have been several high-profile murders of Gypsy and Traveller people that we believe were racially sparked. One fifteen-year-old Irish Traveller boy was kicked to death in May 2003, in the middle of a playing field in Ellesmere Port, Liverpool, where he had gone to visit friends. Even though witnesses heard the perpetrators saying things like, "Kill him, he's only a fucking Gypsy", the judge at the trial said the attack could not be considered to be racially motivated and only sentenced the killers to four and a half years in prison. We are the last face of accepted racism in Britain.

This prejudice is dangerous, and we have lived with it for centuries. Persecution of Gypsies and Travellers has always been prevalent in this country and across Europe. During the Holocaust, it is estimated that between 200,000 and 600,000 Gypsies were exterminated by the Nazis in concentration camps. This atrocity is known by us as the Porrajmos (or 'The Devouring'). The exact number of lives lost remains unknown, as they were not counted-reflecting the widespread disregard for Romany lives, a sentiment that persists to this day.

Chapter Eleven
Striving and Skiving

Having a bath for us in the 1960s and 70s was an ordeal. Mam had an old boiler to heat the water, and she also used it to boil the tea towels and tablecloths. Many gorjas believe Romanies to be dirty; nothing could be further from the truth. Mam never washed any items that touched food, with items of clothing. She spent hours polishing everything she could in the trailer, and what couldn't be cleaned this way was washed regularly instead. I have even seen Gypsy and Traveller women polishing the axles on their trailers or trucks until they gleamed. My sister and her family lived on a site in Hereford for a few years, and I would often go and stay with them during the school holidays. It amused me that the Gypsies living there treated cleaning almost as a competition. Anyone who didn't partake in this rivalry was looked down on and described as a 'needypek', meaning someone who took no pride in their home or appearance and was usually poor to boot.

We had a tin bath that had to be filled with water from the boiler. Bath night was always on Sundays, ready for the week's schooling, unless a particular event occurred on another day. Weekly bathing was common practice for Gypsies and gorjas alike in my childhood, unlike these days, when most people expect to bathe or shower daily.

Like most teenagers, I suppose, I had trouble getting out of bed in a timely manner. I would hear my mother's voice becoming increasingly agitated and impatient with me as I lay cocooned in the blankets on a frosty morning. I always waited until the last possible moment before springing up and getting dressed as quickly as I could, and then racing out of the trailer into the cold air before rushing into the warm shed, where Mam would have a bowl of hot water and soap waiting so that I could wash my face and neck. After a speedy breakfast, usually porridge or cereal and toast, my niece, Jenny, and I would set off on the half-mile walk to catch the school bus. During spring and summer months, the walk along the quiet, tree-lined country road, with hedges covered in white frothy hawthorn blossom and later brilliant green foliage, was pleasant, although tinged with urgency to get to the stop on time, as the bus driver hated having to wait.

The autumn and winter months were a different story, though, especially in wet weather. I disliked intensely having to board the bus, my hair dripping with water, and my blazer and trousers gently steaming on the journey to school. We refused offers from Mam or my sister to wear any kind of raincoat over our jackets, as we knew we would be burdened with them for the rest of the day.

For a few weeks during a warm late spring month, Jenny and I decided that we would deliberately miss the school bus and skive instead. We planned it immaculately, first opting out of the school dinners we both loved, and then switching to packed lunches instead. This ensured we didn't go hungry on the days we played hooky. We would stop about three-quarters of the way along the road and slip through or, if it was locked and bolted, over one of the five bar gates that opened into the hop yard. We then crept along the inside of the hedge until we reached a position, hidden behind a line of poplar trees, where we could see the bus slow down briefly, the driver taking a glance up the road in case we were in view before it sped up and carried on without us.

We then had the rest of the day to ourselves. Our favourite place to wile away the hours was the river. We would skip down one of the hop rows and across the brook into the nearby wood. We hacked our way through the undergrowth, played sword fighting with sticks we found, or looked for bird nests, marvelling at the different-sized and coloured eggs (being careful not to touch the bird's precious ova in case the mother bird then rejected them) until we reached the river. Once there, we lazed around and spent the time playing games like hide and seek, marbles, which I usually had pockets full of, or we used our penknives to make spears and bows and arrows. We enjoyed enacting our favourite television programmes, such as 'The Avengers', 'The Bionic Man', 'Kung Fu', or if it was Jenny's turn, 'Wonder Woman'. We played as only children born before computers and Smartphones knew how.

Jenny strived to do well in education but was not academically minded. In her youth, she had a sunny personality and was emotionally adept at picking up cues from others. However, she had issues with bullying due to her ethnicity too. Some girls could be crueller than boys, and although I did my best to shield her from the malice of some of her peers, she was experiencing a period of intimidation at school and was keen to get out of specific lessons that she found difficult. I had some issues with bullies, but academia held no fears for me. I could do well in exams, even when I had done little studying for them. I didn't worry about having time off as I was fully aware that I could easily catch up on any missed classwork. We began this period of truanting by having one day a week off. I would write our sick notes, changing my handwriting sufficiently enough to avoid suspicion from the teachers; the main problem was that we were fast running out of imaginary illnesses to lie about.

Inevitably, however, we got greedy, and eventually, after a few weeks, we were taking days off at a time. Our downfall came on a day when the weather turned wet and miserable whilst we were hiding, waiting for the bus to pass by. Knowing we couldn't stay out in the open all day if the rain set in, I announced that we would have to go home and claim we'd missed the bus. Worried, Jenny said, "We'll atta wait a bit, otherwise me dad will still be home, and me mam'll make him take us to school!" We agreed to wait until we saw Bill's Cortina go by on his way to the scrapyard where he worked at the time. After watching him drive past us, oblivious to our presence behind the poplar trees, we set out along the road back towards the tan. As we approached the drive that led to our science teacher's house, Mr Zeuner appeared at the entrance to the road in his vintage Land Rover. He stopped and asked where we were going. I replied that we had missed the school bus. "Don't worry," he said, "You're lucky I'm running late and can give you a lift." Jenny and I glanced at each other, our hearts sinking, and climbed into the back seat.

On his drive home at the end of that day, our teacher and neighbour spotted Mam and my sister Mary walking home from the hop garden, where they had spent the day tying the young hops to the rough string that was strung from the ground to wires above, used to support the plants that are akin in looks to asparagus. He said he hoped it was okay that he had given us a lift to school that morning as we had missed the bus.

Mam and Mary gave each other puzzled looks before thanking Mr Zeuner and saying that it was fine and that they were grateful to him. Mary remarked to Mam, "That's funny; Chris and Jenny left in plenty of time to catch the bus this morning".

Mr Zeuner then said that he hoped the family was now all over the sickness bug that had kept us off school the week before. Mam's mouth set in a firm line before replying, "Yes, we're all fine now, thank you for asking".

When we arrived home, Mam and Mary were waiting for us, with knowing looks on their faces. My sister asked, sounding innocent, "Did you have plenty of time for the bus this morning Jen?"

"Oh yes, mam," Jenny replied. But the looks on Mam's and my sister's faces instantly told me we had been caught out.

"You liars!" Mam shouted, disbelief at our brazenness in her voice.

My sister added, "I'm telling your father when he gets home mind, Jen."

Jenny and I were sent to our respective trailers to keep out of the way and think about what we had done for the rest of the afternoon and evening. The period of skiving was well and truly over.

I left Canon Frome School in the summer of 1977 after taking my exams, which I did well in, except mathematics, in which I only gained an average mark. I did exceptionally well in English and several other subjects; however, the exam results went much the way I expected.

Jenny had three years of schooling left, which, for her, had to be endured rather than enjoyed. It also meant that she had to walk the half-mile journey, morning and afternoon, alone. Child abductions in the 1970s were, if anything, even rarer than they are now. Most people didn't give this possibility a second thought. One afternoon, when she was fourteen years old, as she stepped off the bus to walk home, Jenny spotted a car resembling her father's parked in a gateway up the road. Excited to be getting a lift, she quickened her pace but realised as she got nearer that it was not her father's car or him at the wheel. As she passed the vehicle, the side window rolled down, and a man spoke in a friendly tone to her. He asked if she required a lift, but Jenny, who had watched the 'stranger-danger' adverts on TV, declined the offer and carried on walking, thinking no more about it.

The following afternoon, the same car, with the same man, was in the same place at the same time. This immediately struck Jenny as odd, but she was not afraid at this point. As she drew level with the car, the side window rolled down again, and the man once more spoke to her in a friendly, inviting manner. He asked about school, how it had gone that day, where she lived, and whether her parents were at home. And again, he asked whether she wanted a lift 'as it was dangerous to walk alone'. Jenny replied that she would rather walk but thanked him and made to carry on with her journey.

The man then asked if she would like some teen magazines to read on the way. Like most teenagers at the time, Jenny enjoyed reading pop magazines and drew closer to the car to look at the publications through the open window. What she saw was not 'Jackie' or 'Fab208' magazine. Instead, it was hardcore porn. The man leered at her as he flipped the pages to his preferred picture and again asked her to get inside the car 'for a bit of fun'.

Panicking now, Jenny stepped back and looked wildly around for signs of help. She saw my brother Len entering a field with a tractor and trailer in the distance, and just as the man reached out to grab her arm; she fled up the road as fast as she could. She jumped over a gate into the field as the man and his car followed her. She ran without stopping to where my brother was unhooking the trailer from the tractor; looking back, she saw the man slowly driving away.

Len asked if she was okay in a distracted way, busy with what he was doing, and Jenny replied, "Yeah, everything's fine; I just thought I'd come and see you." She was too shocked and disconcerted to tell him the truth. She stayed with Len and got a lift home on the back of the tractor. She knew she should have told her parents about what had occurred, but she didn't. She was embarrassed, ashamed, and worried about being blamed for even stopping and speaking to a stranger. She fretted all night about what might happen the next day and whether the man would be there again.

The following morning, it was raining, and Jenny begged her father for a lift to the bus stop. Although it meant he would arrive at work early, Bill agreed and let her sit in the car until the bus arrived. Finally, during lunchtime, the thought of the man being there again when she got the bus home was too much for her to bear, and she reluctantly told her favourite female teacher what had happened.

My sister and brother-in-law first learned about the incident when the police and teacher brought Jenny home in the late afternoon. From that time onward, until she left school, her father drove her to a different bus stop, where she could wait with other children, and collected her every afternoon.

Years later, in 1995, I was visiting my sister and her family when the first reports about Fred West and the now notorious murders he and his wife Rose had committed were shown on the television evening news. As Fred West's picture appeared on the screen, the colour completely drained out of Jenny's usually rosy cheeks; she stood staring, a look of horror on her face, with the iron she was using held in the air.

I asked if she was alright, and she replied, "That was him."

"Who?" I asked.

"The man in the car that time," she said.

My sister and I looked at each other, then at Jenny, who was now shaking, all of us realising that her escape that day in the summer of 1978 had been fortunate indeed.

Chapter Twelve

Prejudice and Party Games

The bread van would arrive at our tan three times a week. The van, driven by 'Dick, the baker', didn't just bring freshly baked bread that was still warm and smelled heavenly. It also carried a superb selection of cream cakes, crisps, savoury pastries, and the all-important Corona pop. This, of course, was in a period when the name Corona represented something good. The van came on Tuesdays, Thursdays, and Saturdays. If we were not at home, Dick would leave our usual order in a lidded wooden box outside our shed. No one worried that the goods might be stolen, and they never were. In those days, there seemed to be an innate sense of decency and honesty, which appears to be sadly missing in modern society.

Although prejudice and racism towards Gypsies and Travellers was prevalent in my youth, it was certainly not as overt as it is today. Anonymous keyboard warriors now have an opportunity to express vile filth with little or no consequences. These hate-filled people are reticent to express their bile towards the Black or Asian communities: fear of prosecution and disapproval from the press, general society, and governments limiting their actions. No such limitations exist for our communities, however. We are fair game. Rarely is there any positive representation of Gypsies and Travellers in the press or on television. Many of our people have come to accept this, and some try to have as little contact as possible with gorjas. Others have attempted, with varying degrees of success, to integrate and, in some cases, assimilate. Those who choose the latter have to hide their ethnicity and deny their heritage in order to be able to live without the often daily abuse that marks the lives of the majority of people of our ancestries and culture.

Romany Gypsies have lived in Britain for well over six hundred years. Our bloodlines go back to the Uttar Pradesh area of India. In 1530 Gypsies were forbidden to enter England under Henry VIII.

Those already here were deported. In 1554, Queen Mary of England passed the 'Egyptians Act'. This meant that simply being a Gypsy was punishable by death, as was being found in 'the fellowship or company of Egyptians'. This is the only time that fraternising with an ethnic community has been punishable by death, usually by hanging. From 1660-1800, English Gypsies called themselves Romanichals, and we survived by working for trusted non-Gypsies who knew and protected us. However, throughout this period, British Gypsies were still regularly being shipped to the Caribbean as enslaved people.

Appleby Fair, still today the largest Gypsy gathering in the world, was granted chartered fair status in 1685 by James II. Appleby garners a lot of press attention from publications and news agencies worldwide, but little of it is favourable. The press uses tactics such as photographing the site at the end of the three-day fair before the organisers have a chance to put in clean-up services. Pictures of a cleaned-up site hold no interest for them and doesn't fit their stereotypical view of our culture. Many gorjas held hackneyed opinions about us in the 1960s and 70s, but insults were more internalised than said directly.

Several houses on Yarkhill Farm were mainly tied cottages owned by Major Steadman, the farm's owner, and rented to the farm workers for a nominal sum. The Major was generally known as 'Hooky' behind his back due to his large, hook-shaped nose. He liked to dress in shades of green, including a shirt and tie, whilst wearing sweaters with epilates on the shoulders as if he were still in the army. He was old school and believed in keeping the status quo and people in their place.

The Chalk family lived in one of the tied cottages; the father was employed on the farm, and one of the children, Sally, the middle child, was at school with me but a few years older. The older sister, Hetty, would often be seen riding around on her moped. The Chalks decided to throw a birthday party for the youngest child, Ron, and I was invited along with several other kids from the village. The year was 1971, and I was ten years old. We played party games like pass the parcel, musical chairs, and blind man's bluff. Hetty, who was around eighteen years old, was in charge of keeping order and ensuring that the play didn't get out of hand.

We ate sandwiches with the crusts cut off, strawberry-flavoured jelly, blancmange, crisps, sweets, chocolate, and birthday cake. During one of the games, I forgot that we were supposed to let Ron win, as it was his birthday. When I eventually succeeded in the ballgame, Hetty, looking daggers at me said, "You couldn't let him win, could you, you little gypo!" The room fell silent, everyone knowing that this was an insult that should not be used, especially to a child. She looked slightly ashamed as Sally glared at her in a way that said 'you shouldn't have said that'. Hetty then continued, "What? I meant Egyptian."

I knew that she meant every word, however. My cheeks grew red, and I bit down hard, not wanting to show anyone how upset I was. After a few minutes, I said that I wanted to go home and thanked Ron for inviting me to the party. I tried hard not to look at Hetty, and when I did glance in her direction to say goodbye, I noted that she could not meet my eye. I didn't speak to Hetty again until many years later when we met as adults through work. She still couldn't look me in the eye, I observed.

My brother, Len, was as handsome as my sister Mary was pretty. Len had no problems garnering girlfriends. His first real love was a blonde, long-haired, beautiful Romany girl called Ruby. They looked spectacularly good together. Len, wearing his sharp, sixties, Beatle-inspired suits with highly polished winkle picker shoes, and Ruby in her miniskirts, short chic jackets, and knee-length boots. They looked the epitome of 1960s style and fashion. They fell very much in love and got engaged; Len bought her a stunning diamond and sapphire engagement ring that Ruby wore with pride and love.

Sometimes, in our culture, as in most others, it doesn't do to stand out from the crowd too much. Romany culture is, all too often, based on how things look. Some people like to show their wealth and good fortune in a gaudy, flashy way. The more ostentatious the trailers and trucks, the better, for many Gypsies and Travellers. Others like to wear multiple gold rings, bracelets, and chains as an outward sign of prosperity.

Len and Ruby didn't need to brag or be showy. They had something that couldn't be bought. What made them stand out was their style, good looks, and love. These are things that are hard to compete with.

You either have them, or you don't. The people that don't, and even some that do, if they are so minded, can harbour jealousy and resentment towards a golden couple like Len and Ruby. Even though they were both proud of their culture and where they had come from, they didn't look like typical Gypsies, and they were a couple that got noticed when they walked into a room.

Mam and Dad thought the world of Ruby. She spent many weekends with us, and when they dressed for an evening out, Mam would gaze lovingly at them, pride glowing within her, wanting nothing more than happiness for the couple. Some other members of the local Romany community, including some family members from both sides, did not feel the same way. A rumour based on a lie established in jealousy started: that Len was having an affair with Hetty Chalk. Certain people propagated this lie for their own ends, and around 1971, after courting for three and a half years, the engagement came to an end. Ruby returned the ring to Len, and a couple of years later, married another man and quickly had two children. The marriage was not a happy one; it only lasted four years before Ruby left her husband and children and moved into a property in Hereford alone.

Many felt that she never got over her romance with my brother, and he still has the engagement ring she returned to this day, indicating how strongly he still feels about her. My brother had started seeing another girl, Harriet, who was some years older than him and whom I liked immensely. Harriet spent a Christmas with us in the early seventies, one of the rare ones where it actually snowed, bringing a magical quality to the celebrations. Len was not ready to move on from his former love, though, and the relationship floundered after almost a year.

Ruby began having some mental health issues that included deep depression. This culminated in her tragically committing suicide by throwing herself in front of a train just before Christmas a few years later. Many believed that the failed romance with my brother set her on the road to her heartbreaking demise. Len learned of Ruby's death whilst at the annual holly and mistletoe sale at Tenbury Wells, Worcestershire that many Gypsies and Travellers, including my family, attended as sellers of traditional Yule tide decorations. Gypsies and Travellers would buy holly and mistletoe from farmers, making wreaths with the holly, and bundling up the mistletoe to be sold, usually to shopkeepers or market traders who attended the sale as buyers. A lot of money could be made in this way, and Romanies treated it as a seasonal monetary bonus. When an extended member of Ruby's family approached Len and gave him the news of her death, he was devastated and inconsolable, having never really stopped loving her. The results of jealousy and lies are never good, but the untruths that were told and resulted in this dire series of events were both heartrending and heinous in their outcomes.

Len had always enjoyed alcohol, but after Ruby's death, he began to drink in an unhealthy fashion, needing, I believe, some way to block out the pain and obvious grief he felt. His drinking benders would go on for the entire weekend, starting on Friday nights at the New Inn public house in Bartestree, while Saturdays he spent in various bars in Hereford and Sundays at our local, The Newtown pub. Mam and Dad were extremely concerned about his behaviour, as his normal ebullient personality had changed to one of a morose drinker. This behaviour continued for a couple of years before Len met the woman that would return him to the person we knew and loved. Sandra Newman was brash, loud, and could be incredibly comedic, with a wonderful ability to turn a phrase in an amusing way. Sandra was a gorja, but she held no prejudice towards Gypsies and Travellers or any other ethnic group. A divorcee with two children under five years old, she had come from a hardworking family and a complex, abusive marriage.

Len and Sandra met in a pub in Hereford during one of Len's weekend binges. They both saw that the other was emotionally injured, but together, they had a spark that would eventually heal their hearts and psyches. Len kept their romance a secret, even from close family, wary of the judgment that courting a non-Romany girl might engender in the Gypsy community. It came as a total shock, therefore, when Len disclosed one evening, whilst he and I were sitting in my sister's trailer with her and Bill, that he was already married. Mary, Bill, and I were aware that he was seeing someone new, but we had no idea that this secret romance had been going on for a whole year or that Len and Sandra had gotten married the previous Saturday afternoon. What Len wanted now was advice on how to tell Mam and Dad.

Mary and I exchanged eyebrow-raised glances, and Bill's mouth fell open in disbelief. Then Mary declared, "I'm not telling me Mam, she's gonna go divvy."

"How are you going to explain not inviting them to the wedding?" I added.

Len didn't answer, using a shrug of his shoulders to convey that this was a problematic and unusual situation. We still had a few more questions.

"But you took Mam to town last Saturday," I said, "and you brought her home in the afternoon, so when exactly did you get rummered?"

Mary jumped in with, "Did you have a wedding reception?"

Bill sat with a mischievous grin on his face, taking pleasure in my brother's discomfort. "You left your own wedding reception to take your mam home from town," he said with glee, guffawing at his own insight. Len had to admit that this was indeed what had happened. He had got married at Hereford registry office at midday, with only Sandra's family in attendance, and then left the wedding reception at the Game Cock Inn to take Mam home before returning afterwards.

Mary, Bill, and I were shocked and hurt that he had not trusted his family or invited us to celebrate his nuptials. Len tried to excuse his behaviour by saying, "Well, you know what Mam would have said, with Sandra being a gorja."

However, Mary wasn't having any of this. "No matter what Mam would have said, you shouldn't have done that Len," she said with obvious hurt in her voice.

I felt sorry for Mam and Dad; they had done nothing to deserve being treated this way. Mam would indeed have preferred her children to marry within the Romany community, but what Len had done would have repercussions that might last for years. Dad would be put out a bit, but Mam didn't forgive easily and would be incredibly aggrieved.

Over the following weeks, with Len still living at home and Sandra at her mother Nellie's house in Beech Grove, Hereford, a plan was hatched. They decided the best option for not offending Mam and Dad would be to get married again. As far as we knew, there was no law against marrying the same person twice. The second wedding was held at Ledbury register office a month later. This gave the couple time to decorate the farm cottage they would be moving into, just across the green from our tan, and Len brought Sandra to our place to meet Mam and Dad. Mam knew something was up, though. She understood her eldest boy too well not to have picked up on the vibe that lies were afoot. She began to question Len first, then, getting nowhere, moved onto Mary, before, three days before the wedding, she finally got the facts out of me.

The truth, as expected, caused ructions. Mam sulked, and then rowed with everyone, including Dad, accusing him of not caring enough when all he was really trying to do was calm the volatile atmosphere. She stated categorically that she would not attend the second wedding and forbade Dad to go either. Although Mam and Dad did not participate in the second marriage ceremony with the rest of the family, Len persuaded Mam to attend the 'reception' held at the newly decorated cottage Len and Sandra had moved into. Dad didn't need much persuasion, as his nature was always more forgiving.

Mam's reservations about Len getting rummered (our word for getting married) to a gorja divorcee with two children were put to bed somewhat by the children themselves. Kerry was four years old and an engaging and bright boy, and Shelley was a pretty blonde-haired little girl of two. Dad loved them both straight away, and Mam's resentment at the lies Len had told and the fact that he had married outside of the Romany community, she realised, could not be held against the two children, or indeed Sandra. Furthermore, she was impressed with her new daughter-in-law's work ethic. Sandra could work as hard as Mam and was not afraid to get her hands dirty. She was sporty and fit, with a strong competitive streak. Sandra had been a good athlete in her youth and had competed in the Javelin competition in the 3A's amateur sporting event, narrowly missing out on a place in the England team at the Commonwealth Games due to injury.

Len and Sandra's union often blew hot and cold throughout their years together, but there was never any doubt about their love for each other. Sandra rescued Len from the grief and sadness of losing Ruby, and he, in turn, saved her from an abusive relationship and became a warm and caring father for Kerry and Shelley. Sandra discovered that she had cancer of the cervix a year after getting married, requiring a hysterectomy. She and Len both felt saddened because they were unable to have children together, but by this point, Len thought of Kerry and Shelley as his own, and their family already felt complete.

Sandra could always find humour in a situation and didn't mind the joke being on her. During her first marriage, she lived in Birmingham, and whilst out having coffee one day and being heavily pregnant with Kerry, she noticed a shop opposite the cafe with blacked-out windows, into which many men were shiftily going in and coming out again a little later carrying brown paper bags. Intrigued, when she left the cafe, she walked across the road and bent down, as best she could eight months into her pregnancy, and opened the letterbox and peered inside. As she did so, the owner of the sex shop, thinking it might be kids being nosey and that he would have to shoo them away, opened the door, and Sandra literally rolled inside. Looking down at her and seeing the size of her belly, the man said sarcastically, "I think it's a bit late for us to help you, love."

Sandra thanked him for helping her up and then, red-faced, quickly made her exit.

Chapter Thirteen
Pocket Money and Pestilence

For many years, Uncle Aldy drove an Austin A40 van. It hardly ever broke down, and Aldy rarely needed to take it further than Peter Davies's Farm, at Claston, or to Hereford or the local pub. Aldy had lived with us for most of my childhood. When his faithful old van eventually gave up the ghost, my uncle, for some unfathomable reason, chose to purchase an Austin Allegro as his next car. The Allegro was ugly and had some strange aesthetic quirks, such as a square steering wheel. The car was not as faithful as the old A40, and it had several issues that had to be rectified almost from the time he brought it home, with only the delivery mileage on it.

Uncle Aldy was always generous with me; I knew I could rely upon him if I needed extra pocket money. Most kids at the time, including me, had to do chores to earn any additional funds they needed. Dad's family could not read or write. They had spent their youth on the road, with little opportunity to get any schooling. Any writing the family required fell to me, and I quickly realised I could 'earn' extra pocket money this way. Three of Dad's siblings worked at Shawle Court Farm, and each week, I would be called on to complete their work timesheets. Uncle Herbert had a stutter, and it was frustrating waiting for him first to formulate his thoughts and then stumble to get the information out promptly. I would wait patiently for the words to drop into place as Uncle Herbert struggled to control his speech.

The process could take some time, as Herbert also had his sister's work information in his head, and I completed their timesheets too. The time spent doing this weekly 'chore' was well spent. It ensured that our family spent time together, made me feel important as the person who provided this service, and gave my parents another reason to be proud of me. I liked it when Mam and Dad gave me looks of admiration. Indeed, all of Dad's family recognised the benefits of education and regretted not being in a similar situation themselves, as they all shared a fierce intelligence and would have undoubtedly done well had they had the opportunities in education that gorjas often took for granted.

In 1976, something came to Herefordshire that was both unwelcome and meant that Uncle Aldy would no longer be able to live with us. Claston Farm, where my uncle was employed for most of his working life, was the first farm in the county to become infected with the soil-borne hop disease, Verticillium Wilt. No chemical treatments can prevent this, and strict hygiene is necessary to minimise the likelihood of introducing the disease into hop plantings.

Verticillium wilt had been around since the 1950s, but Herefordshire had stayed infection-free up to this point. It was a serious disease that could decimate established hop gardens that had been growing and producing crops for up to twenty years. Once identified, Verticillium Wilt must be grubbed out, and the site of infection must be laid fallow under weed-free grass cover for several years. This could be ruinous for farms dependent on hop harvesting, like Claston, or ours. It could be up to seven years before infected farms could plant hops again. Later years would see the development of resistant hop varieties, but these often produced more minor crops, and some varieties favoured by brewers almost disappeared.

Aldy had to travel daily between Claston and our tan. This meant there was a strong possibility of introducing wilt onto the farm where we lived. Major Steadman, very aware of this, came to our tan and explained to my uncle that he could not continue living with us. Even though troughs of disinfectant had been placed at all field entrances, and everyone was required to dip their shoes or wellingtons into this, the risk was considered too great. Uncle Aldy would have to move. I was distraught. Aldy was always my favourite uncle, and I loved him very much. It hurt that I would no longer be able to see him daily.

After Steadman had left, Jenny, who had been listening to the conversation alongside me, remarked, "Well, that's one 50-pence pocket money gone, Chris." I loathed the fact that she seemed pleased about this but hated more that she had reduced my relationship with my uncle from one of love and respect to one of a monetary incentive. I would have gladly given up all my weekly allowance to keep my uncle with us. Aldy never showed anything but kindness towards me. He was good-hearted, and I felt comfortable in his presence, picking up no negativity from him with my empathic abilities, just an occasional sadness that appeared to come mainly from a sense of loneliness that sometimes washed over him.

Aldy laughed at Jenny's comment but, seeing how upset I was, said, "Don't worry, boy. You'll never want for luvver while I'm around."

This annoyed Jenny, who had a thirst for wealth, but it upset me more, as I wasn't concerned about losing fifty pence pocket money but about my beloved uncle moving away and living alone. "I'm not worried about the vonga," I replied, "I just don't want you to go."

"Where will you go?" I added.

"I'll go to the bungalow," Aldy said.

My grandfather had purchased property and land at Withington many years before. Multiple members of the family had lived there in various times of need. They would continue to do so up until the time my brother and I sold the property and ground after inheriting it as adults following my Aunt Louise's death in 2006. Aldy lived alone in the property at Withington for quite some time before our circumstances changed, and we took our trailer and joined him in the early 1980s. Due to the prevalence of hop wilt in the county, and on Claston Farm in particular, my uncle was not allowed to visit our tan for several years after leaving. We saw him infrequently, either at the pub in Newtown or when he visited his siblings under the cover of darkness at Granny's Tan; although my grandmother had passed over by this point, it was still known as Granny's Tan.

After a few years, Verticillium Wilt had spread to most of the farms in the county, with only a few remote ones escaping. Birds and animals are no respecters of regulations or disinfectant troughs. It was inevitably only a matter of time before the disease spread, forcing hop farmers to rethink their business plans. Many began growing crops such as the brilliantly coloured oil-seed rape, which changed the face of the countryside as we had known it. Gone were the gentle, warm corn colours and the shade creating light to dark green dappled leaves of the hop gardens, and instead came the vivid, artificial-looking yellows of the oil seed that created gaudy patchwork effects across the landscape.

My mother didn't follow fashion. She dressed from a time that was long gone. Her shortest skirt fell to just below the knee, mostly hanging to calf length. Mam favoured check cloth skirts, or trousers if working on the land. Jumpers or knitted short-sleeved blouses topped off with headscarves, or more often worn as a neckerchief, with mainly flat shoes, completed her dress look. Mam's hair only changed once in my lifetime. Unlike most middle-aged or older women, Mam wore long hair. She fashioned a kiss curl on the left-hand side held in place on her forehead, with a mixture of water and soap. The rest hung to the middle of her back, which she pulled back in a ponytail secured with various hair clips and occasionally a rubber band.

The impressive thing about her hair was that she had very little grey in it, apart from a small patch that appeared on the right side above her forehead after she had placed her hand there in shock upon learning of her brother Joe's death. The rest of her hair kept its colour until well into her eighties. When I picture my mother, she hardly changes throughout the years. Her brilliant blue eyes, shining out, were complemented by her tanned features and dark hair. I was shocked the day Mam declared that she was going to the hairdresser. Mam had never changed her hairstyle before. There was a sense of reassuring constancy about her that, as a child, I found very comforting. She appeared utterly different when she arrived home, with her long locks shorn to shoulder length and hanging in ringlets and waves. She looked beautiful. Her hair seemed thicker and even more luxurious, and the grey patch was gone.

However, Mam worried that she had made a big mistake and that she would not be able to maintain the style. I thought it suited her perfectly; she looked radiant, and I loved how the style framed her face. Mam wasn't sure, though, and it only took a few ungenerous comments from her workmates to cast doubt in her mind. One particularly vicious comment from a woman who lived in the village, and who Mam disliked intensely, was, "You must be on the hunt for a new man, Betty; I wonder what Len will think of that?" It seemed that I wasn't the only one that jealousy and resentment followed around. Mam took this woman's enviousness, who herself had thin, mousy white short hair, very much to heart, and washed out the perm and immediately returned to her old styling.

I felt sorry that Mam had done this. "Why, Mam?" I said. "That old mort was only jealous; you shouldn't take any notice of her."

However, what other people thought was important to Mam – too important. I've since noticed that this is a trait shared by many Gypsies and Travellers. How things look to others, and reputation and standing within and to some extent outside of the Gypsy community, matters. I think that for people of Romany heritage, this might go back to our roots in Indian culture. Perhaps the hangover of the caste system is still ingrained within us. History, after all, is not easy to escape, especially for us.

I've often wondered what it is about us that many people hate and distrust so much. It is undoubtedly true that some Gypsies have lived outside of the law or society's norms, but we are not alone in this. The same can be said for every culture. There are always a few rotten eggs in every batch, but we are the only ethnic group where everyone gets tarred with the same prejudiced, racist brush by the majority of people. Those outside the community have a wide variety of racial slurs that are regularly used against us in the English language. In our language, the Poggardi Jib, we don't have any racially motivated put-downs or abusive terms for settled non-Gypsies. We use the word gorja, which simply means someone who is not a Gypsy or Traveller; it is not derogatory and is no different from saying someone is French or Spanish.

Negative views of Romanies and Irish Travellers are still prevalent and, if anything, getting worse. People always need scapegoats, and governments are no different. You don't have to look hard historically to find evidence for this. Difference is frightening for many, and fear, coupled with hate, leads to appalling acts of cruelty, especially in times of war or hardship. Gypsies and Travellers are among the most marginalised groups, and we are regularly sacrificed as offerings in the press, often to distract from the disgraceful actions, and more often, non-actions, of governments here and across Europe in particular.

To some extent, the problem with corruption is worldwide. The current lack of integrity that permeates all political institutions, from local councils to governments, damages us all and distraction politics is commonly used. People in positions of power and influence like to capitalise on this, and Gypsies and Travellers provide the perfect opportunities for our leaders to use dog-whistle tactics, which then influence the majority of the people for political gain.

Chapter Fourteen

Love, Light, and Laurel and Hardy

In 1970, I experienced my second stay in hospital. I was nine years old and attending Withington County Primary at the time. During a playtime session, I somehow managed to fall off a low wall onto an empty school milk bottle. Margaret Thatcher had yet to cancel free school milk, and 'milk time' happened in the first morning break of the day and was looked forward to by almost all of us kids. The bottle broke, and a tiny sliver of glass entered my left thigh. The sliver was so tiny that there was hardly a mark or any blood from the injury. Counting myself lucky not to have been seriously harmed, I continued the morning play and thought no more about it.

Several weeks later, a large abscess appeared on my left leg, just below where the forgotten sliver of glass had entered. The lump was painful and tender, and Mam, worried, took me to see the doctor at Tarrington surgery. Dr Oakland had been our doctor for several years after taking over the practice when Mam's favourite physician, Dr Hargreaves, had retired. By this time, the lump was the size of a small hen's egg, and Dr Oakland announced that he would lance it. I didn't like the sound of that at all and liked it even less when I saw him take a scalpel off a tray under his desk. The doctor first sprayed my upper thigh with a substance designed to freeze the area and then asked Mam and me to wait in the waiting room for fifteen minutes whilst it took effect. A large fish tank took up one end of the room, filled with various brightly coloured fish and objects like sunken shipwrecks and treasure chests that occupied me while we waited. When we re-entered the doctor's office, I was feeling extremely nervous; Mam did her best to reassure me and stayed with me the whole time.

Dr Oakland asked me to lie on my right side on the examination table and insisted that I look away and not at what he was doing. I felt only a light tickling sensation during the procedure. He lanced the abscess, and Mam said later that a lot of dark-coloured blood and pus came out. The doctor stated that he couldn't see the sliver of glass that he thought was causing the infection but hoped that the lancing might have solved the issue. It didn't. Within a week, the abscess had grown again, even larger than previously, and was now the size of a duck egg.

Dr Oakland said that this would probably require a small operation, and I was quickly admitted to Hereford Hospital. The morning after I arrived at the hospital, I was wheeled on a trolley to the operating theatre. Mam and Dad waited anxiously in the room provided. When I entered the operating theatre, a strange calmness came over me. I suddenly realised that there was nothing I could do to change this situation.

The doctors and nurses surrounding me uttered words of comfort that were hardly needed, as a feeling of security was welling up within me. The anaesthetist placed a mask over my nose and mouth and asked me to count backwards from ten. I don't remember getting to seven before I slipped into unconsciousness. As I did so, it was as if I'd stepped into another realm and entered a room that appeared to be filled with beings shaped in human form but made of pure light. I had the peculiar feeling of knowing but not recognising these people.

One being was whispering to me that everything was going to be alright and that I should not concern myself about what was happening. The others appeared to be interested in the procedure, and me, and welcomed me the same way you would an old friend. I experienced a sense of belonging and well-being and felt entirely at home in the radiantly illuminated space. I have no idea how long the operation took, but it felt like I'd been in this place, filled with love and warm, bright light forever. The next recollection I have is of waking up and crying. Mam kept asking me if I was in pain, but I shook my head. I couldn't explain to her that the reason I was crying was because I wanted to be back in the place of warmth and light, surrounded by the beings I both knew and at the same time didn't know. Mam asked one of the nurses to explain what I was trying to describe, and the nurse replied, "It's the effects of the anaesthetic." However, Mam didn't look convinced, and looking back, neither am I.

I spent some time off school following the operation and filled my days discovering Laurel and Hardy on morning telly and reading books in the afternoons while Mam catered to my every whim. Laurel and Hardy are probably my all-time favourite comedians. What I loved most about them, and still do, is their comic genius, apparent good-natured and affable relationship, and lifelong friendship. Oliver Hardy's looks straight to the camera and his physical comedy are legendary, and Stan Laurel's genius lay in his comic timing and the understanding that they were better as a double act than individually. I still watch their films regularly and find them life-affirming and hilarious.

As an adult, I would find a similar partnership with my songwriting, recording, and performing partner, Les Scarrott. Les also understood that we had that essential something together that neither of us had alone. He has often written amazing songs for me to sing lead on when he could easily have kept the best material for himself. Les, like Stan Laurel, tried to serve the craft rather than the ego, although there have been times when I know he has struggled with resentment if my singing was praised too highly or too often. This is not unusual in musical partnerships; Paul Simon frequently walked off stage while Art Garfunkel sang 'Bridge Over Troubled Water' (not that I am comparing myself with Art Garfunkel, whose voice was of a different class, world-class, in fact). Even though Paul had the recognition of writing the song, he still craved the adoration Artie received when singing it.

However, this new normal of lazing around watching TV and reading comics all day didn't last, with Mam saying one day, "That's it, you've spent enough time lying about now; it's time you went back to school." And with that, everything returned to normal, and I had no further trouble from the lump on my leg, which had disappeared and been replaced by a six-inch scar that, although much less noticeable, I still have to this day. Every time I touch it, though, I am transported in my mind back to the place of warmth and love with the beings of light.

Chapter Fifteen
Fairs and Thoroughfares

My first visit to a Gypsy horse fair in 1970 was an eventful one. Horse fairs were prevalent all over the country in my childhood and were well attended by Romany Gypsies, Irish Travellers, and often gorjas too. Our nearest fair was the biannual Stow Fair, which is one of the few still happening today. The fair is held in Stow-on-the-Wold on the nearest Thursday to May 12th and October 24th; it could be the Thursday before or after the charter day. The abbot of Evesham appealed to Henry I in 1107 for official recognition of the market in Stow, which was readily granted. Stow has a unique position at the convergence of eight trackways, making it perfect for trade development. Romany Gypsies and Irish Travellers, and traders from Wales and the West and from the Midlands and the Thames Valley would pass through, ensuring the fair flourished. Gypsies went to show, and buy and sell horses, and to meet up with family and friends. In a time before telephones were commonly owned, it was a significant opportunity for social gatherings, and many young Romanies met their future partners at these events.

It was essential to keep your wits about you when attending this Gypsy Fair, as horses were paraded and trotted through the narrow streets to show them off to their best advantage, and the pavements were packed with onlookers. Carriages were also raced through the streets, and care had to be taken not to step in the path of the oncoming horses and vehicles. The thoroughfares were packed with a vast array of stalls selling a wide variety of goods, such as clothes, horse brasses, blankets, rugs, and fine china and ornaments. Hundreds and sometimes thousands of pounds worth of goods were bought and sold, and horses were exchanged for huge sums of money.

I had never seen so many Gypsies in one place at the same time before. Gypsies and Travellers, like gorjas, come in all shapes and sizes. Some are loud and gregarious, others more reserved, but for all, family is important. Family pride and honour are features that are prominent in our cultures. For Romanies, I believe that this is due to our Asian heritage, where respect and reputation are an integral part of our tradition. Family feuds are as common in our communities as any other.

One of the ways disputes can be settled is by fighting. This was far more usual in previous times, but less so now. Gypsies and Travellers, like everyone else, have moved on with their thinking; using fights to settle quarrels and misunderstandings is no more prevalent in our culture now than any other. It still happens occasionally, however. In 1970 for some Gypsies it was the preferred method, and brought with it prestige for the winner and their families.

My sister, Mary, and her family attended the fair with Mam, my brother, Len, and me. Dad was the only person not to attend, as he couldn't get the day off work. Len and my brother-in-law Billy were most interested in the horses, as both owned some themselves and were keen to know what prices the horses were fetching. Mam and Mary, with me and Jenny in close attendance, trawled around the many stalls, meeting up with family and friends as we did so. Extended and close family members were greeted warmly, some not having been seen for many years. Tears of joy at these reunions flowed abundantly, and the atmosphere was celebratory and cheerful for the most part.

We had just finished our fish and chip lunch, and I needed to go to the toilet. Mam pointed me towards the public convenience across the road and instructed me to come straight back to where they would be waiting for me when I had finished. The convenience had no entrance door, just a walkway leading into the main un-roofed building. As I entered and walked around the corner to find the urinals, I was confronted with the sight and sound of two Gypsy men arguing. Within seconds it seemed the argument escalated into physical violence, with the older of the two men punching the younger in the face.

I forgot about my need to urinate and ran back to my family, saying excitedly, "Two mushes are couring in there."

Len and Billy arrived at this moment from the same direction as me and said they hadn't seen anyone fighting. Suddenly, a crowd gathered quickly in the nearby field across the road. Soon, what seemed like hundreds of people were standing in a circle around the two men, effectively creating a boxing ring for the combatants, who had now both stripped to the waist. Len and Bill climbed onto the stone wall that separated the road from the field to gain a better view as many more people entered the field in an attempt to see what was happening.

Despite my mother's protestations, I, too, managed to clamber on top of the wall, enabling me to see what was going on. The two men were warily circling each other, their fists raised in fighting mode, whilst several other men and women were ensuring that the thronging crowd were kept at a safe distance, securing the 'ring' and making sure the two fighters had enough room to manoeuvre. After each opponent threw half a dozen blows, the fight ended abruptly. An older man grabbed the arms of both fighting men and insisted that they shake hands. The men did as instructed and walked away through the crowd, chatting like nothing had happened. Everyone else dispersed quickly and returned to the usual fair business.

It transpired that this sort of fight outcome was pretty typical and enabled both of the men and their families to keep their honour, ensuring that neither side 'lost face'. This is incredibly important for many Gypsies and Travellers, and long-running feuds could be settled, allowing both sides to move on with their lives without the worry of family pride and honour being damaged. Instances of fighting being used to resolve disputes have reduced dramatically within our community over the intervening years, but for some families, it still has its place.

Horses, traditionally, have played a big part in the lives of many Gypsies and Travellers. They were, and still are, valued as an income for the horse traders, but our relationship with them goes deeper. Just owning and being close to horses is important for many Gypsies and Travellers. In the time of Gypsy vardo's being in regular use, keeping your horses in top condition was essential. My mother and father and their siblings would often have to 'puv out the grois'. This means, in our language, tethering the horses on a grass verge on the roadside and staying with them while the horses rested and regained their strength for the next part of the journey. If no stream or river was apparent, someone usually had to approach a gorja living nearby to fetch water for the animals. It was Mam who was mainly dispatched to do this, as she could easily disarm a surly man or woman with her brilliant, beautiful smile and natural friendly manner. They would sometimes be required to stay with the horses overnight if the grass verge or field was some distance from the atchin' tan (stopping place). Mam never minded this, and she and one or two of her siblings would readily volunteer for the task, keen for a little taste of freedom from the eyes and views of the family.

My brother kept many horses that he traded over the years, but there was one in particular that Mam took a liking to. She was bought as a young filly and stayed with us for the rest of her life. Mam named her Silver, which was an odd name, considering that she was what we referred to as a coloured horse, meaning she was white with brown patches. Silver, who became known as 'Old Silver' was a beautiful mare, and she and Mam appeared to have an affinity and friendship based on love, which emanated from both horse and human. Silver had only one foal, so she could hardly be considered a breeding mare, but this did not matter to Mam.

Even after we moved into a house in the mid-1980s, Mam still found stabling for Silver and ensured she stayed near the family, where Mam could visit her several times a week. Although my brother Len owned Silver, everyone in our family knew that she was Mam's mare, and Len never disputed this. Sandra regularly rode Silver and came to love this horse as much as Mam did.

For the last few years of her life, Silver was stabled, with access to an adjacent green field, at Mrs Payne's property at Southfield Farm in Canon Frome, which was only a hundred yards from the house where

Len and Sandra were living. She could be visited daily by them and the children, with Mam seeing her favourite horse every weekend, always making sure that she took Silver some carrots or a new hay bale.

Silver was part of our family from 1971 until 1988. She was seventeen years old when the inevitable telephone call came from Sandra, saying that Silver could no longer stand and it was time to let her go. Mam insisted on being with her and was holding Silver's head, talking quietly to her when, on a sunny midweek day, the vet put her down. The whole family was distraught, but Mam was bereft. It was as if she'd lost not just a member of the family but a link to her past that could never be restored.

Chapter Sixteen
Presidential Premonitions

I was able to talk to Uncle Aldy about my experiences with the unseen world in a way that I felt I couldn't with my parents. I knew that they would believe me, but it would also bring about some apprehension in them. Aldy never minded my musings and would sit listening quietly to me, occasionally asking for clarification if what I'd said was too vague. After Uncle Aldy moved to our family home in Withington because of the Verticillium Wilt issue that affected more farms over the months and years that followed, I missed him terribly. I had always been close to my uncle and admired the way he said little but thought a lot. When he did pass comment on a subject, I found myself listening in a way that I sometimes didn't to others.

As a teenager, I often felt that the older generation didn't understand modern life or ways of thinking and that 'the old ways' had little to do with me. I now realise, of course, that we are all products of our history and family experiences, and the more aged I become, the more this becomes apparent to me. None of us can escape our past or its effects on us. Even when we try to distance ourselves from painful memories, they have a way of creeping into our subconscious, remaining hidden until the opportunity arises for them to come to the fore. An unkind word or harsh look can sometimes stay with us for a lifetime, especially if we don't want them to. When I spoke about these issues to Uncle Aldy, he would remind me that it was necessary to remember the good as well as the more painful things, that it was essential to keep a sense of balance, and that all things pass, even when we don't want them to.

After leaving school in 1977, I was employed for a short time at Yarkhill Farm, where my family had lived for over twenty years. We were fortunate to have such a place to live. Many other Gypsies and Travellers either still travelled regularly, finding being on the road increasingly problematic due to the reduction in traditional stopping places and limitations from government and local authorities being put in place, or living on sites, either privately or local authority owned. An increasing number were choosing or were forced, through circumstances, to move into housing and live alongside gorjas.

A number of our relatives had chosen to do the same as us and were settled on farms, working for the farmers, and were still able to continue living in their caravans around the Herefordshire countryside. My cousin, Michael, and his family lived on the next farm over from ours at Garford Farm, and I would visit them regularly, walking along the country lanes and through the hop gardens to get there. Michael and I knew we could not continue to live the same lives our parents had. Neither of us felt satisfied or fulfilled working on the land, and because of our education we realised that we had different options open to us. Michael went on to have a career in the NHS and was employed at Hereford Hospital for almost all of his working life.

Uncle Aldy and my parents knew that I could walk roads that had been closed off for them and access opportunities that had not previously been open for most Gypsies; such is the advantage of gaining an education. I applied successfully for the position of trade counter assistant at a builder's yard in Hereford but knew that I would have to move closer to the city, as I did not drive then and public transport was infrequent. The answer was to move in with my uncle at the bungalow in Withington, which had an excellent bus service. Mam and Dad were fine with this as they knew Aldy would look out for me. Mam called in twice a week and always brought food with her to ensure we ate well. I enjoyed living with my uncle but didn't enjoy the job. It didn't inspire me at all, and I quickly moved on to a succession of different roles, including shop and factory work, although none of them held any genuine interest for me either.

It was during this period that my brother and Sandra also had an opportunity to move on. When Mr Ashwin (the manager at Yarkhill Farm) retired, my brother thought he would be the natural successor for the manager's position and would step into the role he was well qualified for. The owner of the farm had other ideas, however. Major Steadman, probably due to his background in the armed forces, believed in keeping people in their place. He allowed my brother to manage the business for an interim period of several months but then appointed a man from outside the area to take over. It was soon clear to us that the new manager didn't like Gypsies. He didn't say anything overtly, but his prejudice came across in subtle ways. He always ensured that my brother had the worst tasks and didn't take Len's recommendations and experience into account at all. Mam said that she didn't like how he looked down his nose at her as if he smelled something distasteful.

Sandra was upset that Len and our family were being treated in such a manner after so many years of service and tried to persuade Len to look for other opportunities. Len was reluctant to do this because he knew that the Major would probably ask Mam and Dad to move off the farm if he took another job and moved away. Several months later, Thomas Hawkins, who owned a large farm at Castle Frome, approached Len. He knew that Len was the chief hop dryer at Yarkhill and wanted him for his expertise. He offered him a position on his farm that came with a larger house and an increased wage. Len went to see Mam and Dad and explained that he wanted to take the job, saying, "You know what this will mean? Steadman will want you out!" Dad told him not to worry and to take the job. Dad knew that they could always move to the family property at Withington when the inevitable eviction notice came, which it did, but not until almost a year later.

Mam and Dad moved to Fernleigh bungalow, which had three and a half acres of land attached to it, as well as an extensive garden that easily accommodated the Vickers trailer that Mam and Dad continued to sleep in, and where Mam still displayed all of her ornaments and chinaware. Mam insisted that they put their names down for a council property, however, as she wanted independence from Dad's family, who may at some point need to live in the property if they ever found themselves in the same position of eviction from the farm they were stopping on. Aldy was delighted that we were together again, and we lived comfortably for five years in Withington, using the bungalow as the living area and the trailer for sleeping for Mam, Dad, and me, as we had previously with the shed on the farm.

One night in March, 1981, I awoke from my sleep with images of a very vivid dream imprinted on my mind. I could not return to sleep, so I got up early and went into the bungalow to wash and make breakfast. Uncle Aldy was getting ready for work but noticed that I seemed out of sorts and asked me what was wrong. I told him about the dream, in which I'd seen what appeared to be an important man, who I thought was a politician, being shot as he was getting into a limousine; he was surrounded by security guards who were all running in different directions. Aldy looked at me and said, "Keep your eye on the news." Then he left for work.

That evening on the 30th of March, as we watched the evening news, we saw the images of President Reagan's attempted assassination just as I had described it. Uncle Aldy said to Dad, indicating his head toward me, "He told me this would happen this morning before anything had been on the telly." Dad nodded but, as was his way, said nothing.

My favourite uncle would become part of another of my experiences with the unseen world in the later period of his life. Aldy lived alone for some time after we moved off the property some years later. I still visited him regularly, and in 2001, when he was in his late seventies, it became apparent that he was having some cognitive difficulties. It was nothing too serious at first, just some short-term memory issues, and he was still the uncle that I had always known and loved.

I usually called to see him on my way home after spending Sunday with Mam and Dad at their tan in Marden, Herefordshire. By this point, I was living in a beautiful top-floor flat with superb river views in Ross-on-Wye and working for the local authority as a Day Centre Officer for people with learning disabilities. It was a job that I loved and was adept at. My empathic abilities stood me in good stead for this post, as I was able to sense what emotions people were trying to express, even when they couldn't get their thoughts across to others. This enabled me to get in front of any potentially difficult situations that usually emanated from the person feeling frustrated at not being understood, and that, for some, could mean emotions being violently expressed.

For this reason, I was often assigned to work with people who were labelled as 'having behaviour that challenges'. I didn't find these individuals challenging, though; they were simply misunderstood. Some of my best, most interesting, and life-affirming moments have been spent in the company of people who many other members of staff found emotionally draining.

On one of my Sunday visits, Aldy and I were having a cup of tea and chatting in our usual amiable way when he mentioned out of the blue that he had noticed some people he didn't recognise in the garden. I looked through the window but could see nothing apart from a slightly overgrown patch in need of some tender care.

"Can you see them now?" I asked, trying to keep my voice light and neutral in tone.

"They've just walked towards the driveway," he replied.

"Let's go and have a look," I said, and we walked out of the back door towards the driveway, where my car was parked in front of the five-bar gate that spanned the width of the lane that was part of the property. We walked up to the gate and, leaning on it, looked at my car and down the lane to the road. "I wonder where they've gone," I said to my uncle.

He looked at me, confusion showing on his face. "Who did you bring with you?" he said, nodding at my car.

"No one, Unc," I replied.

"Then who are the two people in your car?" he said, looking even more confused. I gave my uncle a sidelong glance, wondering if his mental capacity was deteriorating faster than I had previously thought.

"Can you see them now?" I asked, again keeping my voice as natural as possible.

"Yes," he replied, "There's a moosh in the back seat wearing a blue suit and a trilby hat and a young rakli in the front who's smiling and waving at you." I then experienced the by now familiar sensation of emotion washing over me, from my head to my toes, and once again, I didn't know if I was going to laugh or cry. I gazed at my empty car but knew in my soul that what my uncle had stated was true. Even though

I could see no one, every fibre of my being said, 'They are still with me'.

"Yes," I said, "They're waiting for me; let's go back inside; they can wait a bit longer." Aldy appeared to immediately forget what had happened as we walked back to the bungalow, and the conversation returned to normal.

I resolved not to question my uncle any further that day. I didn't want to add to his confusion, and I was still feeling quite emotional. I made sure that he was comfortable and settled before telling him I would have to leave and would see him again soon. He walked with me back to the car and watched while leaning on the gate again as I reversed down the lane. I took care to see that he was heading back to the bungalow before driving off.

I knew that my uncle would not be able to live alone for much longer due to what would later be confirmed as vascular dementia, and I was thinking through the options for him when I suddenly looked at the empty passenger seat next to me, realising that I was not alone. Even though I could not see the other occupants, I could sense they were in the vehicle with me. When I visited Aldy again the following week, I asked him casually over tea and cake, "When I left last week, Unc, did the people you saw go with me?"

"Oh yes, I saw them in the car with you," he replied. "The woman waved goodbye, so I knew that you'd be alright."

I find myself musing more and more, as I get older, on whether people who are in some form of altered state mentally are more receptive to seeing visitations such as this. Most are commonly reported when people are close to death, as I found out from my cousin, Michael, who had experienced this phenomenon during his working life at the hospital. I bumped into him in Hereford a few weeks after my father's death in February 2009. He said he was sorry to hear of my dad's passing, and I said that my only regret was that Dad was alone when he died.

Michael gave me a long look, then with incredible kindness, put his hand on my shoulder and said, "They are never alone when they go." I asked what he meant, and he told me that he had seen visitations at the bedside of a dying person on several occasions and that so had many other members of staff, although most were reluctant to discuss such incidents. I now know that there are many recorded incidents like this from the doctors and nursing staff willing to talk about these issues openly and that several studies have taken place about these happenings, both in this country and others worldwide.

I don't believe these occurrences are limited to spirits in human form, either. The day before my mother passed over in 2010, I visited her in hospital. She was happy to tell me that her cat had visited her in her room. She reported that Tiger had walked into her room and rubbed himself on her legs as she sat in her chair, in the way that cats affectionately do, just as he did when she was at home. I found this poignant, as I had buried Tiger in the garden that very morning, after finding him dead in his favourite sleeping spot, when I went to feed him and check he was alright. He had died comfortably at home of old age after a long and happy life with my mother and father. Mam asked if her cat was okay, and I told her that Tiger was absolutely fine. My mother passed in the early hours of the morning the following day after kissing me goodbye on my cheek for a final time.

Chapter Seventeen

Storytelling Traditions

Mam and Dad's families visited us regularly throughout my childhood. Mam's family members liked to talk about times past and would reminisce and tell stories from their youth. Her cousin, Gerald, who lived on a farm in Weston Beggard, was a regular visitor as he and Mam had always got on well. Romany history was, and to some extent still is, an oral tradition. Stories and tales are handed down over the generations, and being able to tell a good story is a valuable skill that many Gypsies and Travellers value and are adept at.

One of my favourites was the story of 'Old Spring'. Spring was Mam's lurcher dog. He was much loved and highly prized for his ability to catch rabbits and hares. At various times of the year in Mam's youth employment was hard to find. When land-work dried up, and the price of scrap metal dropped dramatically, the options for earning became more limited. Mam and Dad would fall back on door knocking, known as 'durrukin' or 'going out calling', selling paper and wooden flowers, lace, or, if near to Christmas, holly and mistletoe, as well as sundry other items. Having a dog that could provide a free meal was a definite added bonus.

Spring, a large dog, was unusually fast for his size. His ability to quickly catch several rabbits in an afternoon or evening meant that Mam and Dad could feed themselves and my sister Mary, who was their only child then. Owning a dog that could do this meant that the animal was valued and worth quite a lot of money to other Romanies. Some dogs changed hands for considerable sums. Mam never considered selling Spring, though, he was her dog, and she loved him as a family member, as she did with all of the animals she owned, caring deeply for him.

Mam's affinity with horses and dogs was well known, but animals of all kinds trusted her; it was as if they sensed that she was a kind and loving person who would do them no harm. When Spring got caught in some barbed wire after jumping a fence while chasing down a rabbit and ripped his underbelly badly, Mam spent weeks lovingly nursing him back to total health.

Mam's cousin, Gerald, and many other Romany Gypsy men regularly offered to buy the dog. Still, although Mam thanked them kindly for their interest, she always refused their ever-increasing offers. She occasionally loaned Spring to a family member; however, under strict instructions, no harm came to her cherished animal. Gerald hatched a plan: if he took Spring, kept him safe away from the camp, and pretended that the dog had gone missing or been stolen, Mam might say that whoever found Spring could keep him as long as he was returned safely. Mam was no fool, though, and suspected that a rouse was taking place almost immediately. On the morning of the third day of waiting for her dog to come home, she announced loudly, so that everyone in the extended family camp could hear, that unless Spring was back at the tan by evening, she was going to report to the police that her dog was missing.

Gerald knew the game was up and that Mam would never give up on her beloved dog. In the late afternoon, looking well fed and rested, Spring came lolloping back to the tan and went straight to Mam. Gerald returned sometime later and confessed what he had done. Mam assured him that she knew all along what the game was and that she knew that no harm would come to her beloved dog. She forgave Gerald absolutely, laughing and shaking her head at him, saying, "Did you really think I wouldn't jin what was going on?" Even after his rabbit-catching days were over, Spring was always at Mam's side until he passed at a ripe old age. She spoke of him often with affection and love in her voice, and

I'm sure he was waiting patiently for her when her own time came to leave this earth.

Tales and stories are an essential part of Gypsy and Traveller culture. One of the most commonly reported and told is the legend of Gypsies making the nails for Christ's cross. Apparently, it was a Gypsy blacksmith who was ordered to make the nails that were used for Jesus' hands and feet during the crucifixion and, because of this, Gypsies were condemned by God to wander the earth for the rest of time. There are various versions of this story, and legends like this also play into the stereotypes about Gypsies.

Romany Gypsies have always been said to be able to cast spells or curse people, and maybe some can, though it's more likely that, even if it's true, it's used rarely. Curses are about intention; if someone had used this power, it would undoubtedly come at a high cost to the user. It is the case, however, that Gypsies have used this myth as a way of keeping unfriendly non-Gypsies at arm's length. Fear of persecution from gorjas is still uppermost in the minds of many Gypsies and Travellers, who still experience hate speech all too regularly. It is also the case that there are some Gypsies and Travellers who do have psychic gifts. However, this is true for gorja people too. It might be that Gypsies are more open to receiving messages from the unseen world because of the persecution we have suffered, and that we have more empathy with those going through hardship or grief. Many members of my family do believe in the unseen world, and it's a given that we will meet again after death. I have had experiences throughout my life that I find difficult to explain in any other way.

I enjoyed working alongside my mother, even when I was not too fond of the task, as it allowed me to listen as she spoke of events long past. We spent weeks pruning large patches of blackcurrant bushes during the winter months. I often over-pruned and had to be restrained by my mother from trimming the mature bushes too much. "Steady on," she'd say, "You'll leave us nothing to pick in the summer." Mam worked on the land until well into her seventies and prided herself on her ability to work hard. Romanies are taught that nothing comes for free and that we must be willing to toil to prosper.

After a long day of picking, I have witnessed Mam spend hours using a sterilised darning needle to get gooseberry thorns out of her sore fingers and hands. She would sometimes be soaked to the skin after a day's toil in the sprout patch or half frozen in the apple orchard when gathering cider apples off the ground after searching for them in the long frost-covered grass, with her fingers and hands turning blue from the cold. Mam could make an open fire with ease, however, and it would often be the first thing she did when working in the fields so that she and the other pickers could sit around it and toast their sandwiches at break times. It was mine and the other children's task to keep the fire (or the 'yog' as we called it) going by collecting suitable dried sticks from the hedges and ensuring it didn't go out.

My family is not afraid of hard work, and this goes for most other Romanies I know, which is why accusations of being work-shy, not paying tax, and being inherently criminal in our behaviour, irritate Gypsies and Travellers so much. We see programmes on television about Gypsies on benefits, having lavish lifestyles, and over-the-top weddings, and most of us laugh with scorn at the unfairness of these shows, which generally stereotype and, in some cases, make fun of Gypsies and Travellers. The truth is not considered newsworthy and goes against the preconceptions of the media. It is time for the negative narrative that has been apparent for centuries to be challenged and changed.

Racism and prejudice are dangerous, and it is led from the top of society. MP's regularly stand up in the House of Commons and describe Gypsies and Travellers as a 'plague' or 'scourge' on society. I wonder how many of these politicians have actually met or spent any time with a Gypsy or Traveller? Very few, I believe, and those that have may well not have known it because many of us hide our ethnicities due to the fear of persecution. It seems nothing much has changed in people's perceptions of us in the last five hundred years.

Chapter Eighteen
Daydreams and Dragonflies

During my childhood, in the summer holidays, after the age of ten or eleven, Romany children were expected to accompany their parents into the fields to earn money. Some had to hand over what they earned to their parents, and others, like my niece Jenny and me, were lucky enough to keep our earnings as long as we spent them wisely. I liked to take my portable radio with me so that when strawberry or blackcurrant picking, I could keep up with the music of the day. Whenever I hear Steve Harley and Cockney Rebel singing 'Come up and See Me', or David Essex crooning 'Hold Me Close', I'm instantly transported back to the sights and aromas of the strawberry patch, or the apple orchard, or the hop garden. I loved strawberries and sometimes ate more than I picked, resulting in what we called 'the strawberry rash' on our skin, itchy raised bumps that looked like hives. We knew it was time to stop eating them for a while then. Sometimes, we would pick in the morning and then join the gorja children and spend the afternoon playing. I especially enjoyed walking through the corn fields, watching the golden crop moving gently in the breeze, like waves on an ocean. The breaths of wind appeared to whisper the secrets of the countryside, if one cared to listen.

Insects were abundant, and car windscreens would have to be regularly cleaned to remove the debris of dead bugs that hit the glass almost perpetually when driving along. I've noticed that this rarely happens today, indicating the reduction of insects and, consequently, birds and a host of small mammals that were once bountiful. When my mother was a child, maybugs, that my mother called 'whirligigs', which are actually noisy giant flying beetles sometimes known as doodlebugs, were so common that children would attach cotton to them and watch them fly around in circles before letting them go. Hedgehogs are almost extinct, and grass snakes and stoats are incredibly rare. Birds, butterflies, moths, bees, and dragonflies have drastically reduced in number, as well. Everyone seems to be removing the hedges that supported so much of our wildlife, replacing them with six-foot-high wooden fences, and dividing our gardens, not just from the animals but from each other.

Children no longer spend the day playing outside, discovering what nature is about, but instead are holed up in their bedrooms looking at screens, divorced from the natural world. Thankfully, many Gypsy and Traveller children are still encouraged to spend time outdoors, gaining the health benefits that this lifestyle brings. Coupled with a lack of money, imagination is a powerful tool that helps children learn to be self-reliant and content. We spent whole days collecting glass pop bottles from neighbours in the village or hedgerows where they had been discarded and filling up a pram that we wheeled to the local shop in Tarrington to get the money from the returns. This was recycling in its purest form, limiting the need for all of the plastic that is now finding its way into our rivers and streams and polluting the oceans.

The journey along the quiet tree-lined road that ran alongside the river from Yarkhill to Tarrington was full of wonder for us as children. We would stop on the river bridge and watch the kingfishers fly like bolts of brilliant blue under the bridge and down the babbling river Frome. Ducks paddled lazily along, and occasionally we saw otters, which were later replaced by the menacing mink that had escaped from fur farms. We heard cuckoos and woodpeckers regularly, and sometimes, we were lucky enough to catch sight of them, marvelling at their size and, in the case of the woodpeckers, their brilliance. Moorhens and pheasants appeared to be everywhere, along with wild deer and the badgers that could often be seen exiting their dens at twilight.

I still walk the road from Yarkhill to Tarrington at least twice a week when exercising my dog, but I rarely see or hear many of these animals anymore, apart from the pheasants, which, if anything, seem more abundant than before. Raptors, especially Buzzards and Red Kites, also seem more widespread, whilst smaller birds like Wrens and Dunnocks appear to be fewer in number. I used to see swallows coming back and using the same nests year after year, but this is much rarer now. Maybe this is a naturally changing occurrence, but it doesn't feel like that.

I spent hours lazing and daydreaming down by the river opposite St. John the Baptist church in Yarkhill, which was only a few hundred yards walk from our tan, close enough that I could hear Mam calling when it was time to return for a meal. It was while in moments of reverie that I often had thoughts that appeared to come from outside of myself, like knowing the sex of my sister's second child before she was born or that a relative we hadn't seen for years was going to visit us or was ill. I was proven right about these things time and again, and a stage was reached in the family where what I predicted was accepted as fact for much of the time. I learned not to tell my mother of impending portents if they were worrying. Mam would say, "You shouldn't have thoughts like that, my boy" as if having the thought itself could make the bad thing happen.

The long hot summer days in the holidays were spent by the river if I wasn't earning money in the fruit fields. I liked to sit and watch the water swirling past, sometimes fashioning a makeshift rod, or using fishing nets that had usually been won on a stall at the fair, which filled the streets of Hereford for three days during the first week of May each year, to catch fish before returning them to the water. My niece and I were always keen to attend the fair and usually went on a Wednesday, which was the main and busiest day, often meeting up with friends from school.

Sometimes, on weekends or school holidays, my friend Phil, who lived in Tarrington, would ride his racing bike and meet me by the river bridge, where I would be waiting astride my orange chopper bike. We would cruise down the length of Watery Lane and back again, ending up at the river, where we discarded our bikes on the bridge and paddled and splashed around in the water or swam in the height of the summer months. Phil was the only school friend that I hung out with outside of school. He knew that I was Romany, but it mattered not at all to him. We were satisfied simply being in each other's company, hanging out, busily doing nothing in particular; as teenagers are want to do.

We often spent late afternoons together, taking sandwiches, sweets, and bottles of pop or Coca-Cola so that we didn't have to return for tea; instead, we stayed out until the sky changed to twilight before heading home. One or both of us always made sure that we had cigarettes. Our friendship was comfortable in its nature. I admired his easy-going personality and that he didn't care what other kids thought of him. He was contented in his skin and was one of those people who always looked good, regardless of what he wore. Clothes just hung on him well, whereas I felt that I had to work at looking good or stylish.

One evening, after a sweltering and sweaty afternoon, that we had spent mainly in the water or lazily smoking on the riverbank, the time came for us to go home, both of us being under strict instructions to return before dark. We walked, wheeling our bikes beside us, chatting about whether 'Starsky' was better than 'Hutch', or which pop star was the coolest, Bowie or Marc Bolan, along the track from the bridge, with the river on one side of us and Yarkhill moat on the other.

As we approached the road opposite the church, we both stopped dead in our tracks as we witnessed a man walking quickly across the end of the path. What surprised and astounded us was that we could only see the man from the waist up. He wore a brown jacket and a flat cap, and we could tell that he was walking from the movement of his upper body, but he appeared to have no legs, almost as if he was walking in a ditch or that the end of the path was on a different level.

Phil grabbed my arm and said, "Did you see that?" I replied that I had. We looked at each other in amazement, and Phil asked, "Have you ever seen anything like that before?"

I responded affirmatively, nodding slowly.

"I've gotta go," he said quickly, and I immediately regretted my admission as I watched him peddling away along the road, desperate to be home before dark.

When we saw each other at school the following week, we didn't discuss what we had seen for several days; Phil kept his distance and chose not to sit next to me as he usually did in lessons for a while. Eventually, our relationship returned to normal, but he never wanted to speak about what we had witnessed, closing down the conversation if I tried to bring it up. When we met up after that incident, he made sure to leave well before the sun went down.

I don't believe that what we saw was a spirit; instead, it was like watching an image on television. I think that's the difference between ghosts and spirits. Spirits are living entities, but ghosts are recorded moments in time, projected or broadcast into our awareness.

Chapter Nineteen
Bells and Visitations

I am not alone in my family in having experiences of both ghosts and spirits. Many family members can relate similar stories. It is an accepted part of our culture. My Uncle Tommy has a wealth of these tales. Tommy is Mam's half-brother, although she never made this distinction; whether full blood, half blood, or stepbrother or sister, Mam treated everyone the same. They were all referred to as brother or sister. She had a soft spot for Uncle Tommy, seeing similarities in him with her eldest brother Mushy, who she lost tragically in the 1940s.

Tommy and my brother, Len, are actually near in age and spent much of their childhood together. They remained close, and their relationship was more akin to brothers than of uncle and nephew. I liked talking with Uncle Tommy, who is an actual uncle to me, because of our age difference. He was amiable with a good sense of humour and a decent, honest man who, with the love of his life, Aunt Carol, had worked hard to create a stable, loving environment to raise his three children. Whenever I spoke with them, I referred to them as Aunt Carol and Uncle Tommy. I did this out of respect, illustrating that, like my mother, I made no distinction between what we know as the three families.

One of my favourite stories that Uncle Tommy told so well is about the night he spent with my grandfather (his father, Jeremiah), even though my grandfather had been dead for several years at the time of the event. Uncle Tommy loved his father deeply and missed him terribly after his passing in 1964 when Tommy was still in his teens. Due to the way his eldest son had died, my granddad always urged Tommy not to cross water when drunk. This was so ingrained in my uncle that he found it difficult to cross bridges, sometimes feeling a physical weight upon him when he attempted to do so, especially if he had been drinking.

When he was still living with his mother and siblings in the black and white cottage he had grown up in at Weston Beggard, Uncle Tommy often walked to the New Inn public house at Bartestree on Friday nights for a drinking session after a long week of work on the local farm. When he was usually quite drunk, the journey home took him down the winding country road, past the many hop yards and corn fields that he had spent the week working in. Although a slightly longer route, it meant that he could avoid passing over a river bridge that he found so difficult.

On this particular night, Uncle Tommy had drunk far too much cider and left it later than usual to make his way home. He wound his way unsteadily down the road with a flagon of cider in both his jacket pockets and a packet of cigarettes that we call tuvs in his breast pocket. To avoid falling into the brook that ran along one side of the road or the hedge on the other, Uncle Tommy was weaving his way down the middle of the road. Feeling very inebriated and tired and still some way from home, Uncle Tommy heard a voice speak to him, saying, "Oi! You've had a good skin full tonight, ain't ya?"

Turning slowly and in an unbalanced manner, Uncle Tommy saw a man standing behind him. "Yes mate" he replied, in his usual affable way, "Would you like to join me for a drink and a smoke?" he continued, producing one of the cider bottles and showing it to the man.

"Let's sit here on this grass verge," the man replied, indicating a comfortable spot next to the tall hedge. They both sat and Uncle Tommy handed the man one of the bottles and opened the other himself. Maybe because he was so drunk, Uncle Tommy found it challenging to focus on the man's features but felt no trepidation or fear associated with this encounter. In fact, the opposite was true; he felt comfortable and calm in the man's presence.

They chatted as if they were old friends, drinking the cider and smoking the tuvs for several hours. Every time Uncle Tommy lit one up, he handed another to the man sitting beside him. At some point, my uncle was so tired and drunk that he was close to passing out; before he did so, the man said that it would be best if Uncle Tommy slept where he was and didn't attempt to go any further that night. He told my uncle that it would be fine, as he would stay with him and protect him from any harm. It was then that Uncle Tommy realised he was sitting next to his father, not the older form of his dad that he had known, but a younger, more vibrant version of him, just as his father would have appeared in his youth. Uncle Tommy slept soundly on the grass verge until the next morning. When he awoke, he realised he was late and needed to get home as his mother, Rose, would be waiting for him to drive her to town to do the weekly grocery shopping.

As he arrived at the cottage, the memory of the previous night's events flooded back to him, including his meeting with what he now knew was his father. He told his mother and some of his siblings of the encounter, and Rose listened quietly but said nothing, unlike his sisters, who said that he was simply drunk and had imagined the experience.

A short while later, as Uncle Tommy was driving his mother to Hereford, he stopped the vehicle next to the spot where he had spent the night and encouraged his mother to get out and inspect the grassy verge. There, she saw the imprints in the grass where two people had rested, with one empty flagon of cider where Tommy insisted he had sat and one full one next to it where the other person had been seated. Where Uncle Tommy had sat, there were the butts from the tuvs he had smoked, and next to the other person's imprint were the unlit cigarettes that he had handed to his father.

Rose looked at her son and said, "He will always look out for you, my boy; where you walk, so does he."

Children, no matter how well-behaved, have a way of getting into mischief. We were no different in that respect. Whilst we were not spiteful as some children are, we did have a way of getting into trouble, primarily through inexperience, wilfulness, or just plain stupidity. My cousin Neil from Evesham and his sister Sonia used to spend some school holidays with us. We spent the time foraging and having adventures in the beautiful countryside we were fortunate to be surrounded by.

When Neil set fire to a hedge using a magnifying glass, we tried to explain to my parents that it was simply an experiment that had got out of hand. Mam and Dad were not impressed with this justification, explaining that the fire could have reached the neighbouring houses, causing a major disaster. We were made to apologise to the farmer, with Dad standing behind us to ensure we were suitably respectful.

Similarly, when we climbed up into the belfry of Yarkhill church and swung on the bell ropes, creating a cacophony of sound in the middle of the day, we claimed it was just bad luck that the vicar was bicycling along the road outside at the time. Once again, Dad marched us to the vicarage to apologise.

Bells featured in Uncle Tommy's life too. He lived even closer to his local church than we did. Church Cottage in Weston Beggard, where he was brought up, was literally the other side of the graveyard wall. There was never any chance of sleeping in on Sunday mornings for him or us. The pealing bells rang out loudly and proudly for much of the morning. After he married Aunt Carol, and they had their three children, they were stopping in their caravans on a patch of land near Ledbury that was owned by the farmer he was employed by at the time. Three of his siblings, Mary, Amelia, and Sybil, were also married, leaving just his youngest brother, Nelson, living at home with his mother, Rose, who had moved out of Church cottage into a council house just up the road by this time. Granny Rose and Nelson lived at No 6, Weston Beggard Lane, for many years and were well-liked and respected by their neighbours.

In the summer of 1981, Uncle Tommy took his family to Pembroke for the summer potato picking. He had just purchased another trailer for his daughter to sleep in so that she had her own space and didn't need to share a trailer with her brothers, as all of his children were now in their teens. One Friday afternoon, they were in the fields and looking forward to the end of a hard week's potato picking. The whole family shared the strenuous, physical work, as was the way for most of the Romany families that laboured at the Welsh resort during the summer months. Uncle Tommy was nearly at the end of his potato row when he glanced up and saw what he thought was sea mist rolling over the ground towards him, almost as if it were a living thing. As he stood up, stretching his stiff back and easing his tired muscles, the mist stopped and rose up in front of him, taking the form of his mother before disappearing as quickly as it had emerged. Shocked, he stumbled backwards, and Aunt Carol grabbed his arm and asked him what was wrong.

"Can you see that, Carol?" he exclaimed, wonder and fear in his eyes.

"It's just mist, Tommy. Whatever's the matter?" she replied.

"I saw me mam in the mist," he said, his voice filled with bewilderment and astonishment.

Concerned, Aunt Carol insisted that he go to the public telephone box and contact his mother's next-door neighbour, Mrs Gwillam, one of the few people in the village to have a telephone at the time.

When Uncle Tommy called, the neighbour asked him to wait while she fetched his brother, Nelson, to the phone. Uncle Tommy waited with a growing sense of unease. When Nelson came on the line, he told Uncle Tommy that their mother was acting strangely and didn't seem like herself at all. My uncle said he would return home the next day. He packed up quickly and, after settling his family back at his tan near Ledbury, went to see his mother immediately. When he walked into the house, he was surprised to see that most of the furniture was missing and that his mother had packed everything she owned into boxes.

"Whatever's going on, old woman?" he asked gently.

Rose looked at her son and said in a steady voice, "My time here is nearly done, but I won't die in this house. I shall die as I have lived for most of my life: in a trailer."

Uncle Tommy didn't argue or ask any further questions. "Well, you'd better come with me then," he said. "We've got a spare trailer that I bought for Tina; you and Nelson can have that."

The last items that Granny Rose removed from the house were pictures of her dead husband and stepson, both called Jeremiah. "They have never left me since they passed," she said, "and I won't leave them now." She took the pictures off the wall in the front room and carried them both out of the house and up the path without looking back.

Every evening for the next week, Rose walked along the fence at the edge of the piece of land where she was stopping with her son, and she rang a bell for a few minutes, all the while looking into the wood that bordered the land as if expecting to see a face she knew all too well walk through the trees to greet her. Rose knew that bells were regularly used by mediums in the 19th century at séances to attract spirits.

"What are you doing that for, old woman?" Uncle Tommy would ask, but Rose would simply say that she was waiting for someone. "Who are you waiting for?"

She only replied, "I'll know him when I see him."

Granny Rose died from a heart attack in Aunt Carol's arms in the trailer she was living in eight days after walking out of the house at Weston Beggard. Just as she had predicted, she died as she had lived for most of her life: in a trailer.

Chapter Twenty
Copper Cans and Tin Churches

My mother spent hours cleaning brass. She had an extensive collection of kettles, candlesticks, vases, dishes, and horse brasses. I think she used this activity as a kind of mindfulness where she could escape the day's worries. She often stated that dull brass was shameful and ugly. Her favourite pieces had pride of place in the trailer, including a pair of copper water cans that came from India in the 1950s, which she bought in 1968 from an immigrant who was a blanket and rug seller. They were handed down to me, and I still have them. They look as good today as they did the day she purchased them and are now proudly displayed in my front room. Many admirers have offered me large sums of money for them, but I have never been tempted to sell. I can feel Mam's love and dedication whenever I touch the copper handles. I enjoyed watching my mother rub off the Brasso with the soft cloths she used to clean the items, and I occasionally helped her with the task.

She was engaged in this activity the day her cousin Gerald came to tell her that my grandmother, Rose, had died. Mam and her stepmother were incredibly close, and Granny's death affected her deeply, as yet another link with her beloved father, Jeremiah, had been lost. I don't think it matters how old we are; when we lose our parents, we suddenly feel orphaned. Even when we have our own families around us, we are still alone in that moment. It was the only time I saw my mother faint. I managed to catch her before she hit the floor, saving her from injury, but Mam was extremely distressed. I had not seen her so upset since she had received the news that her brother Joe had been killed when I was a small child in the 1960s. Granny Rose's funeral was a large affair, as is often the case with Romany Gypsies. She was buried with my grandfather at Weston Beggard church, next to the cottage where she had lived for so long and had raised five of her children. On the day of the funeral in August 1981, as I stood next to my mother looking down at my grandparent's grave, I had the strange feeling that I would somehow hear from my granny again when the time was right.

In 1993, I was employed by my local authority as a day centre officer at The Ryefield Centre in Ross-on-Wye, Herefordshire. I made several lifelong friends whilst in my term of employment there, as well as a few enemies who were jealous of my success in climbing the promotion ladder. During my time there, I was invited by a colleague, Jennifer, to attend a spiritualist meeting in Newport, Wales, which she had heard was worth going to as the medium was supposed to be excellent.

I agreed to attend with her. I had been interested in the subject of life after death (or as some prefer to refer to it, life after life) for some time and had already attended two meetings. We arrived in Newport the following Sunday evening and located the venue without difficulty, which was a small church made out of wood and corrugated tin. The church was well attended and we took up a couple of seats near the back of the room.

The medium led the prayers and hymn singing and then proceeded to give the messages from the unseen world, which was the main reason most people had attended. He was in his late twenties or early thirties and was both interesting and annoying to watch – annoying because he had a Lee Evans, the comedian, style of approach. He was fidgety and couldn't keep still or stand in one spot for more than a few seconds. He spoke quickly, giving a large amount of information in a short span of time. He gave several people messages with what appeared to be a high degree of success. Jennifer and I watched with interest and growing admiration for his skill and accuracy when giving the communications from deceased loved ones.

The carbon copy of Lee Evans then announced that he had a connection for a man in the audience who was wearing brown clothing. Only one other man apart from me was sporting any brown clothing items. I wore a brown woollen sweater, and a man near the front of the room wore a light brown jacket. 'Lee' went straight to the other man.

"Right," he began, "I've got a man here that had a problem with his hip and has a walking stick. He's giving me grandfather energy; I think he was in the First World War; he's with someone else; and why do I keep seeing a rose?" The man in the tan jacket shook his head and, looking confused, stated that his grandfather was still alive and that he didn't understand the rose connection. 'Lee' looked intently at the man and shifted impatiently from foot to foot before continuing confidently. "It's definitely a grandfather, and I'm still seeing a white rose."

By this time, I was once again experiencing the familiar, highly emotional sensation that I had come to know so well from my early childhood experiences. I raised my hand tentatively above my head as Jennifer looked at me in amazement and said, my voice quivering slightly, "Excuse me, I think you should be talking to me."

'Lee' appeared to notice me for the first time. "A man wearing brown," he said, with confirmation. He walked over to me, "Do you have a grandfather who's passed over?" he asked. I admitted that I had. "Was he in the First World War?" he pressed me further.

"Yes," I confirmed. "He also had a hip injury that he got in the war, and he did use a walking stick."

"So why do I keep seeing a rose?" he asked with a tone of genuine interest.

I paused slightly before saying, "My grandmother's name was Rose." This caused a few gasps from some of the other people in the audience.

He stared at me with a satisfied and somewhat relieved look on his face. "Ah," he said, "she's the person slightly behind him, who's now coming forward and is standing next to you. They just want you to know that they are both with you and are watching and guiding you as best they can. She is saying that you are on the right path," he said in his usual fast rate of speech. He reflected slightly, "They are fading now," he stated, "but they are sending you waves of love."

'Lee' moved back to the front of the audience, and I sat back down next to Jennifer, who placed her hand on my arm and mouthed 'Wow' at me, smiling as she did so.

This episode convinced me that I am never really alone; it also ensured that, since that day, I have not needed to search for more evidence of an afterlife. I know there is life after life. I know it as surely as I know that the sun will rise tomorrow, whether I am still here to see it or not. This knowledge is of great comfort to me, as it is to others of faith, regardless of whether they have had similar experiences. I actually admire people who believe without the experiences more. They have a pure faith that requires no evidence and is much harder to achieve.

Chapter Twenty One
Life's Simple Pleasures

My paternal aunts, Louise and Mary, never married. They seemed content to stay at home and look after their parents until they passed over. Whether they were really at ease with this is unknown, but I didn't see any evidence that they bore any resentment towards their parents because of their decision. They both worked on the farm at Shawle Court, Monkhide, where they lived, and didn't travel far from their tan.

Louise was the more outgoing of the sisters and caught the bus into Hereford every Saturday morning to do the weekly shopping. Mam and Louise didn't always get on, although there was no open animosity; Mam felt that Louise cared more about money than she did about people. However, I don't think that's a fair criticism, as I never experienced anything but kindness from either of Dad's sisters. Perhaps they were too similar to be friends.

It's sometimes said that we see in others what we dislike most about ourselves. Many of Dad's family regretted not having any schooling, yet they were extraordinarily intelligent, especially in mathematics. They could all do sums in their heads without any difficulties, and I often got Dad or my aunts to help me with maths homework, not being as gifted in this subject as Dad and his family were.

Aunts Louise and Mary often dreamed of winning Littlewoods 'Spot the Ball' competition and spent hours examining the weekly newspaper picture, trying to figure out where the ball should be. The top prize in the 1970s was £250,000, an absolute fortune then and unimaginable for most people (except Viv Nicholson, who, when she won, declared that she was going to "Spend, Spend, Spend!"). It was the national lottery of its time, and millions of people entered the contest. I've many a time wondered what they would have done with the money had they won, but I'm also sure that they, too, had dreams, just as most other people do. I visited them weekly and was engaged to address the envelope containing what they always believed to be the winning entry. My aunts were never short of optimism.

After Granny Ada died, Louise and Mary remained at home, and although they missed their mother greatly, they appeared satisfied with their simple life and its simple pleasures. Mary was the quieter soul of the two, but she also had the fiercest temper. Small in stature, she was not to be messed with and didn't suffer fools gladly. She had no time for gossip and believed in a live-and-let-live philosophy. She would look at her sister with distaste when Louise returned from the weekly shop full of 'news' and say, "Louie! Is that all you go to that town for? To just stand on street corners, gossiping about people that you don't know?" Louise took no notice of any rebuke and carried on, relentlessly giving the weekly 'news'.

They were very different personalities that generally got along well. They both believed in the unseen world, but Louise was the more pragmatic of the two and the more likely to dismiss signs from the other realm. After Granny Ada passed, Mary reported seeing her mother on several occasions, even though Louise would admonish her for saying so. However, Mary was incredibly honest, and it would not have occurred to her to lie about these visitations. She was not afraid either; rather, I believe she found her mother's visits somehow comforting.

When Mary began having stomach issues in 1985 at the age of fifty-three, she did not immediately rush to see a doctor; instead, she took a 'what will be will be' attitude, which is so common among Gypsies. This attitude is probably partly what accounts for the relatively high death count that is still prevalent among many Gypsies and Travellers, who end up dying at much younger ages than the general population. This is understandable when you consider that Gypsies have often avoided interference from any kind of officialdom, including medical practitioners, due to the inherent racism and prejudice that many of us regularly experience. Prejudice has many consequences, including an early death for those who are subjected to it.

After suffering silently for a few months, Mary was finally persuaded to visit the doctor by her sister, who knew something was wrong. After tests, it was revealed that Mary had bowel cancer. She was successfully treated by having part of her bowel removed, and Mam and I visited her several times when she was recovering in the hospital. She was grateful that her life had been saved but stated categorically that she was not afraid to die. Her belief in the unseen world was unshakable, and I think part of her would have welcomed seeing her parents and loved ones again. She was told by the surgeon who performed the operation that if she could be clear of cancer for the following five years, she would probably live well into old age. Mary smiled and thanked him warmly, but she had a look that said, 'these decisions are out of our hands', and she was simply grateful for any extra time he had given her.

She returned home and went back to work on the farm alongside her sister as she had always done, returning to her life of simple pleasures. Mary and Louie enjoyed plain foods that were still cooked using an ancient black-leaded stove that required regular feeding with coal and wood. It also served as a heater for the timbered hut they lived in. They listened to Radio Four throughout the day when not working and loved watching their favourite programmes on the television in the evenings. Louise planted a variety of flowers in the garden, her favourites being gladioli, which could easily be seen through the windows and attracted bees and butterflies of all kinds. They also grew many of their own seasonal garden vegetables.

One of the reasons Mam and Louise liked to get the early bus into Hereford on Saturdays was to get a good position in the queue for the second-hand clothes market, held in the Percival Hall in St. Owen's street. The queue was packed with mainly women, often of a particular age group, who barged each other out of the way to get to the best items. The competition was fierce, and some of the women attending used whatever methods they needed to employ to ensure they found the items most desired. Elbows were usually the weapons of choice. Sometimes, when small, I was dragged into the fray by my mother, and occasionally saw arguments and even fights break out between the 'shoppers'.

This was usually one of the few times when Mam and Aunt Louise would look out for each other. I have seen both of them step in to defend the other during an argument that involved tugging on a piece of clothing or a pair of curtains whilst hurling insults and shouts of

"She saw it first" at the perceived offender. Mam and Louise would often leave the hall feeling bruised and battered, but with their bags full and smiles on their faces; they would look at each other with gratitude for the support the other had given. After all, family is family.

Dad, too, was a man who enjoyed the simple life; he was calm, contented, and mainly left it to others to get upset about issues. The notable exception was if he felt that he had been unfairly treated. Then, he would set his cap more firmly on his head and stand his ground, regardless of the outcome. It was different if he and Mam disagreed; Mam would want to argue and row with Dad. It infuriated her that he would sit listening, barely passing comment. I once saw her jump onto a basket of expensive crockery, smashing it to smithereens just to get a reaction from Dad that failed to materialise. Dad had worked out early in their relationship that you didn't win arguments with my mother by engaging in them. You won by saying as little as possible.

Dad was the eldest sibling in his family; Mary was the youngest. Despite this, they were the siblings most alike. It was especially worrying for Dad then when he found out that his youngest sister was ill again. Mary's cancer had returned almost five years to the day after her first diagnosis. This time, following the discovery, which I think she had expected, Mary chose to refuse further treatment. Mam, Dad, and her brothers and sister tried to persuade her otherwise, but it was to no avail. She simply said that if it was her time, then she was ready and that she 'didn't want to be cut about again'.

In the last few days of her life, Mary refused to see anyone but her sister Louise, not wanting, I believe, for her family to be upset by her obvious pain. She passed over to the unseen world, lying in her own bed at home with her sister, who she had lived with for her entire life, holding her hand. She died in as simple a way as she had lived, being as little trouble to people as she could.

Chapter Twenty Two
Soul Group Recollections

As a child, I could decide whether or not I wanted to be around a person based on the colours I sometimes saw around them. I learned that this is called an aura and can even be photographed using a Kirlian camera. The people with lighter and brighter colours are usually more manageable for me to be around. I find spending time with people with dark grey, dark reds, or very occasionally black smoky auras more challenging. This ability has faded somewhat as I've got older, but I still experience this phenomenon with some people. I don't see these colours with my eyes, but instead, I see them in my mind, although sometimes it's not easy to tell the difference. The colours can change and fluctuate, too, depending on the person's current mood.

This ability goes hand in hand with my empathic skills. Walking into a room full of people can be overwhelming, especially if the people there are upset or angry. I then feel an urge to escape, which I have to manage by imagining that I am surrounded by the white 'Ready Brek' glow, as seen in TV adverts in my childhood. The feelings, after a little while, often dissipate then. Sometimes, I can tell when people are unwell or in pain using these abilities; this was more apparent to me when I was a child, but again, it still occurs occasionally now. Using these abilities has stood me in good stead when choosing friends throughout my life. I have known and retained most of my close friends for many years, some since childhood. It's also beneficial when engaging with trades people. I immediately get a sense of the person's honesty and reliability, and I have rarely been wrong with my initial impressions of a person. However, this has not stopped me from making mistakes when it comes to issues of the heart. I have had my fair share of failed romances, but I have learned something vital about myself from each of these, and I have never regretted a relationship.

I have spent much of my life alone. There is a massive difference between being alone and feeling lonely. I have rarely experienced this feeling, knowing that we are never really forsaken. The man in the blue suit and trilby hat has always been with me, whether I knew it or not. I have often wondered if I chose to come into this existence to discover what life is like without my soul mate beside me in a physical sense. I believe that we decide our current lives when we are still in the other realm and return here to discern certain lessons and experiences that we take with us back to the unseen world.

When I was in my late thirties, I attended the Cheltenham Literature Festival. One of the events there happened to be a woman doing aura and life readings. She asked volunteers to go up and have their auras read, and I found myself raising my hand in the air. I sat in a chair in front of the audience, and the woman stood behind me and placed her hands near my head.

After a few moments, she said, "Oh, you are quite unusual." I wondered uneasily what information she was about to come out with. "When you incarnate," she carried on, "you do so with a group of people, a soul group, and what's interesting is that you don't get to progress to a higher spiritual level until all of the group is ready to progress." This did not surprise me, and it seemed fitting, as I've often felt that I have known the people who are close to me throughout many lives. "You have lived many times," she went on, "and you will probably live many more, as not all of your group evolve at the same speed; you are here to help those people so that you can all move on quicker."

I wasn't sure how I felt about her last statement, not being sure that I wanted this responsibility or happy that I could relive the same experiences over and over throughout many lifetimes. Some experiences surely only need to be lived through once, especially those that involve loss and pain, either of a physical or mental nature. I realised, however, that we are all different, and progression and understanding are as difficult for me in some areas as it is for others in their respective learning. Ultimately, I found her statements to be comforting and they supported my belief that none of us are truly alone.

When I was in my late teens, I had a very vivid dream. I saw a house made of stone, set into a hillside, surrounded by green fields.

Inside the house, standing next to a large open fireplace, was a young woman. Although she didn't look like my mother, I knew without doubt that she was indeed my Mam. Strangely, a stream of bubbling water snaked through the middle of the room and down the field. This didn't look right at all, and I knew that the stream shouldn't really be there. I awoke with these images firmly embedded into my consciousness. For many years, I could not shake this vision, which would come back to me at certain moments with perfect clarity and in full colour.

Almost forty years later, I was holidaying in North Wales. I was staying, with just my dog Sparky, a rough-haired Jack Russell rescue I loved with all my heart, for company in a cottage near Beaumaris on the Isle of Anglesey. The cottage garden ran down to the beach, overlooking the Menai Straight, on the other side of which was the Snowdonia Mountains. I felt incredibly at home, and the surroundings seemed familiar to me even though I had never previously visited the area.

A few days into my week-long break, I decided to look around the Snowdonia area in more detail. The area is a national park of outstanding beauty, and it absolutely lived up to its reputation. The roads in the region are winding and long, with towering mountains covered in greenery and streams running down the hillsides wherever you look. As I drove slowly along one of the mountain roads, taking in the magnificent scenery and looking for a convenient place to stop and give Sparky a well-deserved walk, I noticed a tumbledown stone cottage set away from the road into the hillside. I immediately pulled over and stopped the car. It was the house I had seen in my dream forty years earlier. I walked with Sparky into the ruins of the house. The ceilings and slate roof were gone, but most of the walls were still standing. I stepped into what would have been the front room and instantly saw the large fireplace I had seen in my dream. I could also see the young woman standing beside it in my mind's eye. I then looked at the 'floor' that was now grass, covered with broken slates scattered all around, and saw a bubbling stream winding its way through the 'room' and out through a gap in the wall, down the hillside towards the road.

I had a familiar sense of déjà vu and knew without question that I had resided in this house with a woman who didn't look like my mother but undoubtedly was. A few images of this past life flooded my mind, and I realised that I had lived, loved, worked, and died in this place. I'm pretty sure that I had been a miner in the area, as whenever I pictured myself, I was covered in soil and dust, not from coal but from copper, which had been mined in the vicinity. It took over forty years for me to understand the meaning of the dream I'd had as a youngster, but this event also linked with what I'd been told by the aura reading woman at the festival in Cheltenham some years earlier. I realise now that the people I know and who are close to me are part of my soul group. We have all played various parts and a range of different roles in each other's lives and will always be connected in one way or another.

Chapter Twenty Three

Furry Friends and Family Feuds

My first dog was called Rex; my sister had rescued him from a dog pound near Hereford. Mary and her husband, Bill, brought him to our tan to meet me on a sunny weekend evening when I was around four years old, and I loved him as soon as I saw him. He was a chunky, short-legged, dark-haired terrier cross with the sweetest personality. He was patient, loved being with children, and went everywhere with me, trotting along happily by my side. He was my best friend and always looked at me with total love in his eyes.

When I started school, and Mam was the nominated parent to accompany us kids, he would walk the mile-long journey with me. If it was another parent, he stood watching until we had disappeared around the bend in the lane. Mam said that for much of the day, while he waited for me to return, he would curl up on my bed or watch through the trailer window. Exactly half an hour before I arrived home, he would get up and sit waiting at the end of the lane until he saw me appear, then he would race up the grass-lined path excitedly and greet me with not just his tail wagging but his whole body, at the same time as covering my face with loving licks.

Our dogs, called jucells in our tongue, were treated as family members. Even working dogs like Mam's lurcher 'Old Spring' were treated with reverence and love. Rex liked to sit next to me whenever he could, always ensuring that one paw was touching me so that, even when he was snoozing, he could tell instantly when I moved away and would quickly follow wherever I went. Dogs are the most faithful companions of all animals. The love they give is unconditional, and they teach us a lot, not least about how to live in the moment. Dogs don't bear grudges and forgive us for any misdemeanours we make.

The same cannot be said for humans. I have known some feuds between Gypsy families last for generations, only usually being healed when one member of the family marries someone from the opposing one. Even then relations can sometimes remain strained. Perceived slights can grow into huge arguments and tensions can occasionally spill over into violence. Usually fights for family honour are staged events, like the one at Stow fair that I witnessed, others can flare up quickly and be over in a flash.

I inherited a copper kettle from my mother that is older than I am, and I clean and polish it as regularly as Mam did. When I do this task I am often reminded by the dent in the side of the kettle of the time when Mam poggered (hit) one of her extended relatives with it during a row one hop picking. She knocked the relative out with one blow of the kettle, bringing the argument to a swift end. I know that Mam always regretted actions like this, but she would never show that regret outwardly, seeing apologies as a sign of weakness.

My sister, Mary, inherited my mother's quick temper. When some Romanies that Mam and Dad still held a grudge against, following an altercation twenty years before, came to our tan one day and started arguing with my brother, Len, over something that he had supposedly said to one of them while out drinking, my sister happened to be in the water-shed washing up and listening quietly to the ongoing and increasingly loud argument.

Suddenly, Mary burst out of the shed door, ran down the concrete path next to the corrugated tin sheds and stood next to my brother. She looked threateningly at the other Romanies before saying, "Don't you come to our tan shouting at my brother, you no good needypeks." My sister knew that the 'needypek' slur would sting as it inferred someone was 'mokadi', meaning dirty and not a genuine Romany. One woman took a step forward, and my sister squared up to her straight away, saying loudly, "If you take one more step, I'll knock you down where you stand." The woman thought for a moment before backing away, and her husband, realising that they had probably taken on more than they could handle, started to make placating sounds.

They left quickly and didn't return. My niece Jenny and I, agog, watched the whole disagreement from the trailer window. Mam was outside throughout the bickering, washing clothes in a large steel bowl; she had said nothing during it, just carrying on, keeping an eye on the unfolding proceedings. I noticed a wry smile on her face as she looked at my siblings, who were standing beside each other with their arms folded, watching the interlopers drive away. I could tell that she was proud of her children for standing up for themselves and each other.

Mary and Len glanced at one another, and Mary said, "That's told them. They won't be back again." Len smiled, and then they both laughed, and all of the previous tension disappeared instantly.

When Rex was around nine or ten years old (we were unsure of his exact age, but he had been with me for six years by this time), there was a summer night thunderstorm. Thunder was one of the few things that frightened Rex. He would cower under the table in the shed, shivering and hiding behind the long tablecloth. He usually slept at the foot of my bed, but this night, he refused to come out from under the table when it was time to retire to the trailer, and reluctantly, I left him in the shed. The wind and rain battered against the trailer as we tried to sleep; lightning flashes followed by raucous claps of thunder carried on for hours deep into the night.

When Mam got up early the next morning, the skies were clear, and bright sunshine illuminated the damp grass and surrounding trees. I awoke to the sound of Mam calling Rex's name. I scrambled quickly out of bed and ran out of the trailer into the shed. 'Where's Rex?' I asked Mam. She explained that when she got up, the shed door was open, and it had obviously blown open during the night, as it was only fastened shut by a rickety latch. Mam assured me that Rex would return, but there was no sign of him despite us both searching the village and calling for him throughout the day. I was distraught, and it upset Mam seeing how distressed I was. I refused to go to school the next day, saying that I had to find him. After three days, though, I was beginning to give up hope, and Mam and Dad insisted that I return to school lest the truancy officer visit. I couldn't focus on anything; I only wanted my beloved dog back. I blamed myself for leaving him in the shed overnight, knowing the door was not secure.

I never saw Rex again apart from in my dreams, where he visited me regularly for years afterwards. Sometimes, I thought that I had glimpsed him out of the corner of my eye, and my heart would jump for joy, but a profound sense of loss always followed it. It was several years later when Mam told me that my brother had indeed found Rex lying dead on the side of the road a couple of miles from our tan. He had been hit by a car, probably as he ran from the sound of the thunder on that stormy summer night. No one in the family had the heart to tell me what had happened, as they knew I blamed myself for his disappearance. I wished they had told me at the time, as I could have held him one last time. I believe that this would have helped in the grieving process, too, but I know that my family were only doing what they thought was best. Over the following years, we had many other dogs, and I loved all of them, but none as much as Rex. In fact, it would be nearly forty years before another dog came into my life that I loved as much as him.

After Mam passed over on the 5th of September 2010 at the age of eighty-nine, I inherited, amongst other things, her terrier dog, Patch. Because I had been renting various properties over the years, I had not been able to have a dog since I'd left home at the age of eighteen. A few years before Dad and then Mam died, I bought a house in the village next to theirs so that I could be close by if they needed me, which they often and increasingly did. I was working full-time as a manager of day services for people with learning difficulties, and the job and my parents' increasing needs meant that I had little time to look after a dog as well.

Patch was a lovely ten-year-old Yorkshire terrier, and just before her passing, Mam insisted he came to me to be looked after. I did this gladly, as I had become very fond of her little dog, which had a feisty personality just like Mam. I cared for him for two years and was surprised at how much I enjoyed having a dog in my life again. When he got pancreatitis and died at the age of twelve, I suddenly felt very alone. I found it difficult when I returned home after a day at work, and he was not there to greet me, with his tail wagging warmly and a look of love in his eyes.

Several months later, I was browsing a website for older dogs in need of re-homing when I spotted a six-year-old; cheeky-looking, brown and white, rough-haired Jack Russell called Sparky, who had just been taken in by St. Giles animal rescue centre in Taunton, Somerset. The look in this dog's eyes spoke to me straight away. That familiar voice, which was not mine, inside me said, 'This is the one.' I rang immediately and agreed to meet him two days later after having a successful suitability check from an animal charity. I drove to the centre, which took a couple of hours, and when I arrived, he was brought out to meet me. The first thing he did was lean into my leg and rub his head against it, looking up at me with soulful, grateful eyes. I took him for a short walk, and when we returned, I agreed to adopt him without hesitation.

The rescue centre had a vet's surgery on site and said that he would have to be castrated first. They agreed to do this the same day and said I could then take him home. He was still asleep from the surgery when I placed him in the dog cage I had purchased from them, and he slept for almost the entire journey home, only waking as we stopped at traffic lights as we entered Hereford. Sparky sat up in the cage and looked out of the windows, in a surprised and slightly worried way. I spoke softly to him, assuring him that we would soon be home and that everything would be alright.

When he entered the house for the first time, he skipped around the front room with what appeared to be absolute joy. Sparky settled in very quickly. He was a loving dog with a character that matched his name. Like Rex, he slept on my bed from the very first night, keeping one paw on me at all times, just as Rex had done. I think people who have not accepted a dog into their lives find it perplexing to comprehend just how much love and comfort a dog can bring to an individual or family.

Sparky went everywhere with me, including on holidays and sometimes to work, especially if I had evening meetings to attend. He would sit on my feet as I prepared food, looking up, waiting for a tasty morsel to drop into his mouth. He was the first dog since Rex that I loved with all of my heart. All I wanted was to ensure he had a wonderful life with me. The only information I had about him was that he had been found as a stray near Taunton but appeared to be well-fed and cared for. I ensured Sparky had a lovely life, and he lived to the grand old age of fifteen.

He had been having heart issues for a couple of years, and when the day inevitably came that his vet said it was time to let him go, I found it one of the hardest decisions I've ever had to make. I insisted that the vet came to the house, and Sparky passed peacefully in his favourite sleeping spot in the front room of our home. I spoke quietly and softly to him the whole time, assuring him that he had been 'the best dog I could have wished for'. He is buried in the garden where he loved running around. I think about him often and am thankful for every moment I spent with him.

Since Sparky passed, I have rescued another Jack Russell, who is just as lovable but whose personality is quite different. Mr Pickle was six months old when I adopted him, five months after Sparky's death, and he has helped enormously in getting me over my grief. I get the feeling that Sparky is still around, though, and just like with Rex, I have caught glimpses of him several times. I even felt him sitting on my feet when preparing a meal one day, and I looked down, fully expecting to see him there. I hope when I pass over that all the dogs I've loved will be there to greet me. This thought always comforts me, even though it brings tears to my eyes.

Chapter Twenty Four

Swallows, Swifts, and Flights of Fancy

Dad often said that he hoped to return as a bird in his next life. He would sit, watching the Swallows and Swifts zooming around, catching insects on the wing, or gazing at the murmurations of Starlings creating complex shapes and images in the sky with a look of wonder and awe on his face. During his youth, Dad had fallen from a horse whilst attempting to break it in and injured his back. This became more problematic for him as he got older, and he found it increasingly difficult to stand up straight for long periods of time.

As the oldest of his siblings, he was tasked with breaking in young horses, more so than his brothers, who Dad believed had a more leisurely ride in life in general. What Dad had that they didn't have, was a brilliant sense of humour and a way of looking at the world that was offbeat and unique. Most people who met my dad liked him. He was respectful of the opinions and feelings of others and genuinely had an interest in what they had to say. He was an avid viewer of news programmes, and he could instantly see when a government minister was obfuscating the truth. He would have had a field day with today's ministers, seeing them for what they really are: mostly people who have been trained in how to avoid answering a straight question.

Following his industrial tribunal win for unfair dismissal, Dad was able to take life at a more leisurely pace. It was during this period that he taught himself to read and write, albeit at a reasonably low level. Dad was a keen learner with a thirst for knowledge, and would have definitely benefited from a formal education, where I believe he would have shone.

He enjoyed learning new words from me, and I loved the way he would mix these newer words with ones that came from a different era and were no longer in regular use, as well as combining them all with the Poggardi Jib. Dad used words such as 'scran' for food, 'a twelvemonth' for a year, 'wench' instead of woman or girl, 'bide' for stay, and 'the morrow' rather than tomorrow. His language was rich in history, and it had an old-world charm that set him apart in an uncommon way.

Dad liked a nap in the afternoons and would fall asleep in his chair with his cap pulled over his eyes and his mouth slightly open. One hot August day during the school summer holidays, as Jenny and I sat watching our new and recently purchased colour television; we witnessed a bluebottle fly into Dad's mouth, followed by him choosing that exact moment to close his lips. Giggling like crazy, we watched and listened to the fly buzzing around in Dad's mouth, wondering if he would swallow it or spit it out. About a minute later, Dad slumped further in his chair, and his mouth fell open again, releasing the fly, which flew quickly through the open door, none the worse for wear. Our laughter woke Dad up, and when we told him what had happened, he said he didn't believe us; he hadn't been asleep and had only closed his eyes for a few moments. We knew differently and continued laughing until Dad also began to laugh before shooing us out of the shed to go and get some fresh air and play outside, not wanting us, I think, to witness his snoozing.

Our first colour television, purchased in the mid-1970s, revolutionised our viewing experience. Ours was a Teleton, made in Japan. It was special because it didn't have buttons that you physically pushed but controls that only required a slight touch of our fingers to change the channel whilst illuminating the button that had been selected. Unlike so many televisions of the day, from the front, the set was hardly bigger than the size of the twenty-inch screen, most of the workings being housed in a box that protruded at the back. It seemed wondrous to us, the colours bringing alive even the most boring programmes.

People born from the mid-1970s onwards have no idea how transformative the invention of colour television was. It was akin to getting high-speed broadband in its day. Westerns, in particular, were a revelation, and viewing in colour made the experience vastly more enjoyable. I remember watching 'Shane' with Alan Ladd and being overwhelmed by the richness and depth of the colours, making it so much more engaging than watching in monochrome.

Mam was only an occasional viewer, mainly of soaps like 'Crossroads' or 'Coronation Street' and only then because it meant she could comment when the other women on the farm talked about the latest storyline during the working day of picking or hoeing, or whatever other farm task they were involved with. Dad, however, loved watching television. It transported him and gave him insights into different lives and places that he knew he would never see in real life, although they fascinated him all the same. Dad watched it all: 'The Sweeney', 'Charlie's Angels', 'Starsky and Hutch', 'Dad's Army', 'Steptoe and Son', 'Love Thy Neighbour', 'Panorama', 'The Benny Hill Show', 'A Family at War', and 'The Good Life', were just a few of his favourites.

He was an astute viewer, too; he knew what was good and well-made and what was dross and not worth wasting his time on. Dad would have made an excellent TV reviewer. He liked to wax lyrically about how his life could have been if he had been born in another country or a different time. These flights of fancy enriched my thinking and let me know that it was alright, even beneficial, to have dreams and to put myself in someone else's shoes and imagine what it might be like to live their lives.

I became fascinated by any programme with a supernatural theme: Friday nights were for watching the late-night Hammer House of Horror movies. Christopher Lee as Dracula is still my favourite interpretation of Bram Stoker's gothic horror. Even when I had to watch through my fingers at the most frightening scenes, I still had to watch. I've wondered, as an adult, if it was the viewing of horror movies, in particular, as a teenager, which led to me not using the psychic gifts that I have had for so long. For many years, from my late teens to mid-thirties, I actively chose not to use my gifts and even rejected them as wishful thinking. I did this until some events occurred that simply could not be ignored.

While working in Geelong, in Victoria, Australia, in 1997 as part of a career exchange, I visited the old and recently closed down Geelong Gaol. The venue was, at this time, being used in a variety of different ways, including parts of the gaol housing an art exhibition area, and the service I was employed by used some rooms as a community base. However, many sections of the gaol were in their original state and kept more as a museum piece.

One evening, whilst attending an exhibition, I wandered off from the main area into the old part of the building. I came upon an iron gate that spanned the width of a large corridor, behind which I could see two rows of cells going back into the gloom. Suddenly, a feeling of fear and dread came over me, as if I was physically being affected by the emotions of the men who had been prisoners there. I experienced all of the hopelessness, anger, and hostility of the previous inhabitants, and the feelings invaded my psyche until I began to feel physically sick. Fearing that I would vomit, I backed away as quickly as I could and returned to the main group.

When I had regained my composure, I spoke to one of the organisers, who had worked at the gaol for several years, and asked him about the cells I had seen and the type of prisoners they would have held. He informed me that those cells had housed the inmates who were destined to be hanged for their crimes, which were of the worst kind imaginable. I think it's possible that stone buildings can hold imprints of the emotions of the people who have lived in them, almost like a kind of videotape, and that feelings and sometimes images can be replayed again and again given the right circumstances. I certainly believe that is what I experienced that evening, and I knew that I would never be able to return to that section of the building again.

The emotions of the former prisoners were, and probably still are, embedded into the very fabric of the building. I just hope they have moved on spiritually and are not stuck in some kind of permanent, repeating cycle.

My parents' relationship was not perfect. It could be stormy occasionally but was always based on a deep love for each other. It was not the kind of love that was overly demonstrative or 'lovey-dovey'; instead, it was based on mutual respect and support. They lived through some of the best times for Romanies and some of the harshest. They had to work for everything they had, often side by side. Their mutual appreciation for each other was borne out of hardship and out of the prejudice and racism that they faced. Still, this support and loyalty was all-encompassing within their relationship and included their children and close family.

After my father passed, my mother found life unbearable. She tried her hardest to keep going, more for our sake than her own, but it was as if she didn't know how to exist without the steadying influence of Dad. His calm, quiet composure balanced her feisty, fiery nature perfectly. Without him, she found it increasingly hard to control her emotions. She often sank into a deep depression that sometimes outwardly lasted for weeks or months but probably never lifted inwardly.

Even though, over the years, I have lived in various cities and another country, I have ended up returning to the area where I was brought up. I regularly walk my dog around the lanes and fields where my Mam and Dad stopped with horses and wagons when they were young. I like to stand still in one of these places on spring or summer days, listening to the birds and insects surrounding me. When I do this, I fancy I can hear my parents' voices drifting towards me on the breeze, as if their spirits still inhabit the places they once frequented. Wherever they are, I know that they are together.

Chapter Twenty Five
Fitting in and Tripping Out

I've had a few recurring dreams throughout my life. The first appeared when I was a young child, not long after starting primary school. The dream involved being chased by a giant old-fashioned penny piece. The penny would appear massive in scale and was on its edge, standing some way off in the distance. It would then roll slowly towards me, growing in size and scale as it did, until each groove in the edge seemed like a monumental trench that I could be swallowed up by. No matter how fast I ran, I could never outrun the penny, which would eventually roll over me before disappearing briefly. I would then stand up, look behind me, and see the penny in the distance once more rolling slowly towards me, repeating the whole sequence. This dream went on for many years, and I'm sure it is linked to feeling overwhelmed in life or not being in control of things. I don't think it's a coincidence that it started when I began school.

I found academic life difficult for the first few years, not because I didn't enjoy it, but because it took me out of my comfort zone and introduced me to gorjas, who thought and acted differently from the adults I had known previously. I learned many new words and ways of thinking. We mainly spoke Romaine at home, but I immediately sensed this was inappropriate at school. Our language is as much about tone and inflexion as it is about different word usage. Gypsies and Travellers have distinctive ways of speaking that is easily recognisable. Often, even when we don't look different outwardly, we are identifiable by our accents and the rhythms of our speech. To survive in the 'outside' world, we have to learn quickly how to adapt our speech patterns and language, simply in order to be understood and to avoid the prejudice and bias that inevitably comes our way as a consequence of our ethnicities.

I have had lucid dreams throughout my life. This is when you become aware that you are dreaming during the dream. It began as a child with the classic dream of falling, in my case, off a cliff. As I fell towards the ground at an ever-increasing rate, I suddenly realised I was dreaming. I recall hitting the ground, which appeared to be made of sponge, and bouncing back up into the air, laughing wildly. These dreams are a bit like how I imagine taking a 'mushroom trip' to be. They present as quite psychedelic and full of colour, the likes of which are not usually seen in the natural world, at least not seen by us, with our limited colour view. I've heard that even a simple goldfish can see more colour spectra than humans. This does not surprise me; humans are limited in many ways, not least in our compassion for others and our planet.

Fitting into the settled community's world is easier for some than others. Those who have attended schools and colleges have had to make the difficult choice of whether or not to disclose their ethnicity. Often, there is no choice, as people pretty much always discover what a person's actual background is. I learned quickly not to tell people too much about my family. The more people knew, the more ammunition they had to use against you. I've seen instances where Gypsy children have been bullied to the point of wanting to commit suicide. This usually happens with the full knowledge of the teachers, and there have even been occasions when staff encouraged it. Fitting in for Gypsy and Traveller children can be a matter of life and death. These are uncomfortable truths for many people to hear, but I've never met a racist who believes they are guilty of racism or prejudice. People can always find reasons that not only excuse but justify their racist stance.

The powers that be like to promote the United Kingdom as a forward-thinking and liberal country, where racism and prejudice are frowned upon and legislated against. Nothing could be further from the truth when it comes to Gypsies and Travellers. Whenever a Gypsy site is proposed to be built by a local authority, the slew of complaints that the proposal receives is extensive and widespread. One of the most common complaints is that a site will reduce the value of nearby people's homes. Think about that for a moment: would this excuse be acceptable if it was aimed at any other ethnic group? If a white person complained that a black family moving in next door to them reduced the value of their property, they would rightly be vilified for their views. Yet it's perfectly acceptable to voice this opinion if it's a Gypsy or

Traveller family moving in or a site is located near the properties of settled people.

Consequently, the few sites that are built are often in places where settled people would find living unacceptable. Sites are located near motorways; train tracks, large industrial factories, sewage works, and on land previously used as toxic waste dump sites. The sites themselves often resemble concentration camps, with high fences surrounding them; in fact, this seems to be a prerequisite for many authorities because God forbid that someone should have to see a caravan, or worse still, an actual Gypsy or Traveller! This says a lot about how people in positions of power think about Gypsies and Travellers, and these views filter down into every aspect of society.

It wasn't always this way, though. As a child, my family lived and worked on a farm, as did many of our relatives. As far as seasonal work went, we made up the bulk of the workforce. Things began to shift in the late 1980s as farming practices changed and required fewer staff. Quite quickly, we, as ethnic groups, went from being valued for our work skills to becoming a problem that no one wanted to address. Many Romany Gypsies had no other option but to move into housing, whether they wanted to or not. Gaining permission to create a private site is a long, arduous, and extremely costly undertaking. Many have neither the funds nor the wherewithal to get through the process, which is extraordinarily complicated and, some would say, deliberately designed in such a way as to be almost impossible.

There are many people in positions of power in this country that don't want Gypsies and Travellers to be integrated into mainstream society. Instead, they want forced assimilation. Some have even called for our protected status as races to be removed to make this assimilation easier. This is reminiscent of the rhetoric used in Germany during the 1930s, leading up to the Second World War. Hopefully, there are people in the settled community and the halls of Westminster who see this for what it is: discriminatory, divisive, and dangerous. What can happen to one group today can happen to others tomorrow, and we must learn from history if we don't want to repeat past mistakes. We will need the support of settled people and other ethnic communities to ward off this jeopardy.

We keep hearing that we are the first generation to know that we are destroying the natural world, yet rivers are still being flooded with phosphates that run off the land into waterways, destroying fish and animal life. The regulatory authorities and companies responsible for this allow it to happen in the name of profit.

Many Gypsies and Travellers are more in tune with the natural world, as we have often lived closer to it, as my family did when I was a child and as many of my kin still do. Few settled people have vegetable gardens anymore, preferring instead to pave over their gardens to create extra parking spaces. I am grateful and fortunate that I grew up in the lush Herefordshire countryside, where I still live and walk daily. One of my greatest pleasures is gathering blackberries and cob nuts in the early autumn months and field mushrooms that taste so wonderful, fried fresh from the field. For Gypsies and Travellers, the land is our garden, and long may it remain so.

Chapter Twenty Six
Red Beads and Reading Wagons

Granny Rose, named Rosina Loveridge, was born in Dunstable, Bedfordshire, where many of her family are still based. She later moved to High Wycombe, Buckinghamshire, where she met her common law first husband and had four children. After her husband was killed in a road traffic accident, Granny Rose and her children travelled in their large Reading showman's wagon (Showman's wagons were well known for their beautiful, intricate, and ornate design) to Toetree Lane, near Stratford, Warwickshire. There, she met Mam's oldest sister, Mimey, and her husband, Nelson Johns.

Granny Rose and Mimey got along well and worked together, hoeing in the pea fields on a piecework basis and stopping near each other. Mimey and Nelson introduced Rose to my grandfather, Jeremiah, who had recently returned to a life on the road after his children had grown up and moved back into wagons with their own families. Widow met widower and fell in love. They were married in Stratford, with Jeremiah's son, Joe, and his son-in-law, Nelson Johns, as witnesses. Their first two children, Mary and Amelia, were born in Badsey near Evesham within the first three years of their lives together.

Mam was thrilled that her father, following the death of her mother, Lavinia, many years earlier, had Rose to love and support him. Rose and her four children were accepted into the family and loved by her six stepchildren from the start. The family was close-knit and travelled and stopped together, often on the same farms or ones adjacent to them, meeting up regularly and looking out for each other. Mam and her elder brother, Mushy, were incredibly close, and one day, he returned from Evesham with a long string of red ceramic beads that he gave to my mother as a present. The string of beads was so long that Mam could wear them as a double string that still fell low on her breast. Whenever I think of my mother, she is always wearing the red beads.

After Mushy's sudden and unexplained death, the beads became even more important to Mam. She would run them through her fingers, gazing into the distance, wondering how the events around her brother's death had occurred. It was an event that Mam could never reconcile or find peace with, and she spoke about it often and with much sorrow. As the years passed the beads became fewer in number, as strings broke, and beads became lost. There came a point during my childhood when the double string became a single string of beads. Mam mourned the loss of every single bead, each one lost, reminding her of the grief and actual loss they represented. But also, with each bead lost came time, and time, whether we want it to or not, brings perspective.

Mam learned to live with the loss of both of her brothers, who each had passed in harrowing and heartbreaking circumstances, and as time went by, the loss of each bead became almost a symbol for the easing of her pain. Granny Rose helped Mam on both a spiritual and supportive level to cope with her grief and loss. Rose believed strongly in the unseen world and spoke about her beliefs in both a matter-of-fact and a knowledgeable manner. The unseen world was as natural to her as the physical world. Death held no fear for her, and she instilled this belief into her children. Rose understood that when you don't fear death, you are truly alive and living life to the fullest.

Chapter Twenty Seven

Miracles and Milestones

Miracles come in many forms: doctors who save lives against all the odds perform miracles regularly, accidents being averted, scientific breakthroughs, miracles of nature, and even life itself. As a teenager, to save on the bus fare, I often hitchhiked into Hereford. I used to walk to the main Hereford to Worcester road, almost a mile from our tan, and stand with my thumb out to hitch a ride next to the milestone marker on the side of the road: Hereford 7 miles. If no car stopped, a midland red bus eventually turned up, and I had to spend some of my precious money on the fare. It was probably a miracle of sorts that I didn't come to any harm.

Milestones, too, come in various forms: the physical blocks of stone placed at intervals along a highway or life-changing events that are usually unexpected and sometimes, though not always, unwanted. Occasionally, miracles and milestones happen simultaneously and change our lives forever in the blink of an eye.

In 2001, I lived in a spacious top-floor flat in Wye Street, Ross-on-Wye. I had been there for several years after moving to be closer to my work in a centre for people with learning difficulties. I loved my role as a day centre officer and made some of my dearest and most longstanding friends during this period. It was at this time that I witnessed a miracle, which also became a significant milestone in my life.

Les Scarrott and I were in the middle of recording our third album called 'Corn Circles'. The title was inspired by our visit to a crop circle in Wiltshire that summer. The formation on Milk Hill was known as 'The Galaxy' and consisted of 409 circles in a spiral of six arms, each containing thirteen circles. It had appeared fully formed after a night of heavy rain in late August and was simply breathtaking in its intricacy. The extent of its size beggared belief. It was possible to stand at one end of the formation and not be able to see its end. The flurry of circles of varying sizes swept around like a vortex, creating a design of great beauty. Les and I visited a few days after its formation, which had been widely publicised in the newspapers and broadcast on TV news. Many people reported strange occurrences whilst visiting the circle, and on the day we visited, it was eerily quiet, with very few people around. I even noticed that the birds avoided flying directly over or landing in the formation. For some reason, the creation had a major effect on me and seemed portentous. Indeed, it was only a few weeks later that 9/11 happened, which changed the entire world irrevocably.

Our interest in the paranormal had been growing for a while. Although I had experienced many occurrences during my childhood and teenage years, I had also dismissed most of them as a young adult, probably due to my interests in work, relationships, and the general concerns of living and surviving. The galaxy formation reignited something within me, and we began writing songs reflecting our growing interest in the strange and otherworldly. I started speaking openly about my previous experiences and, importantly, stopped worrying about what other people thought. I suspect this confidence coincided with maturing and having people around me that I trusted not to ridicule my beliefs and anecdotes.

Writing and recording sessions for the Corn Circles album took place either at Les's tan or my flat. The songs flowed easily, almost as if we were receiving them via some kind of psychic antenna. The writing reflected our burgeoning interest in what some describe as 'high strangeness', including 9/11, which consisted of four strategic attacks, one of which was the destruction of the Twin Towers in New York, killing nearly 3,000 people.

The terror attacks in London some years later further unnerved the nation and the world, and people began to wonder how the new millennium was going to play out. Would these events create more fear and hatred, or would we witness some sort of spiritual revival? For Les and me, it was the latter. We began to look into various forms of spirituality and to discuss what we had read about with our friends and fellow musicians in an open and forthright manner, both of us no longer being inhibited by fear of what others might think. This renewed freedom of thought meant I was increasingly open to receiving messages from the man in the blue suit, which had been so prominent in my early life. I believe that a message, actually more of an instruction from him, even saved my life on one occasion.

On an early autumn day in 2003, I was driving to a gig at the BBC, where I would meet up with the other members of my band, The Brickshed. I was in the middle lane of the M5 driving towards Birmingham. The mid-morning traffic was heavy, and all three lanes were full of vehicles. About two cars ahead of me in the inside lane was a large truck carrying huge underground pipes made of cast concrete. The truck indicated that it was moving into the middle lane, where I was driving at around sixty miles an hour in my treasured Ford saloon car. Suddenly, I heard the man in blue's resonant voice. It said clearly, "Move into the inside lane." I did as requested without hesitation and watched in horrified awe as two pipes moved away from the load ahead of me. The traffic in the inside and middle lanes, including my car, started to slow down; we were all trying to keep as much distance between ourselves and the truck as possible, whilst the vehicles in the outside lane chose to speed up to try and get in front of the truck and alert the driver.

The first pipe smacked into the tarmac, and a car in the middle lane just ahead smashed into it, with shards of concrete of varying sizes raining down over the road. The second hit the tarmac and broke into two main segments. One piece rolled into another vehicle and disintegrated with the force of the impact, whilst the other half flew high, spinning end over end through the air as if in slow motion, and landed on the roof of the car next to me in the middle lane, which was precisely where I would have been had I not changed lanes when instructed to do so.

When I described what had happened to my bandmates later, Les asked me if the voice I'd heard was internal or outside of my head. I thought carefully about this question, but still, today, I don't have the answer. However, I do know that it wasn't my voice, recognising it without doubt as the voice of the man in blue. It was a miracle that nobody was seriously injured, and neither I nor my car had a scratch on us. I was grateful that the man with the trilby hat had chosen to intervene in my life again, but it would not be the last time.

As a child, I was regularly told that if I was rutefull (which means being naughty), then the Muller would come for me and take me away. Mullardi means haunted, and the Muller, my family believe, is a demon spirit akin to the devil who (among other evils) abducts badly behaved children. Evil spirits and those who use the 'evil eye' feature prominently in Romany culture. For instance, Mam would never let knives cross on the table, as this was seen as a sign that an argument would ensue or that mischievous spirits would cause trouble for the family. Belief in the power of good and evil was uppermost in my mind for much of my youth.

My empathic abilities often meant that there were some people that I found it hard to be around, especially those whose intentions were not pure. I could always tell which pupils at school it was best to stay away from; those with anger issues or low self-esteem often lashed out at others who I described as lighter beings, because the light is physically and spiritually hurtful to those who prefer to stay in the shadows of life.

Chapter Twenty Eight
Barton Street Theatre

One of the things the psychic told me was that I was surrounded by jealousy and had been for a long time. Candle blowers, I believe, is the expression; people who think that blowing out the glow of others makes their own dim spark brighten. They are not correct, of course, and if we allow ourselves to be influenced by them, then we all wind up stumbling around in the dark instead of shining as we are meant to.

I hadn't planned to go to Barton Street Theatre in Gloucester that particular Wednesday in 2006. I arrived home from work and flicked through a free newspaper that consisted mainly of advertising, and my eyes were drawn to an announcement of a psychic evening taking place that night. Instantly, I knew I had to attend. I experienced a feeling of sureness that this was the right thing to do wash over me, as if I'd dived into a pool of emotion.

During the drive from Ross-on-Wye to Gloucester, a thought was instilled in me. Something was going to happen, and I had to let it. I don't think it can be the case that all Romany Gypsies believe in the unseen world, but it is true of my family and many others I've known.

There is an acceptance of another existence beyond this one, which we all know and share. The paranormal is just another normal in my family; we have always seen signs where others have not.

Mam never really got over the death of her older brother Jeremiah, nicknamed Mushy, at the age of thirty-five. He had been missing for more than a week when his body was found by a dairyman in the river Avon near Evesham in August 1948. He was discovered on the ninth day after he had disappeared. Several people were questioned about his death, but nobody was charged, and at the inquest, an open verdict was recorded. When my uncle's body was dragged from the water, he was identified by a couple of objects he had in his pocket. A glass eye and silver St. Christopher that my mother, many years later, gave to me. I still have it. My parents always believed that my uncle's death was the result of foul play, as did many others in the local Romany community. The fact that the case was and still is unresolved contributed significantly to Mam's mental breakdown following her older brother's passing.

Uncle Mushy was known for his boxing prowess, and he often competed successfully in Jack Scarrott's travelling boxing booths at various fairs around the country. His brother and sisters refused to watch in case he was injured, all except Mam, who would go with him and stand at the side of the ring holding her brother's coat, ensuring fair play.

For a long while, after her brother died, my mother had trouble sleeping. The last time she had seen my uncle alive was three months before his death, at the May Fair in Hereford. Mam bitterly regretted not being allowed to see his body for a final time. She was prevented from doing so by a police officer, who told her it was better to remember him as he was, insisting she would never be able to get the images of him out of her head after he had spent more than a week submerged in the river.

One night, sometime later, in desperation, she spoke aloud to the unseen world and asked for a sign that her brother was safe and at peace. Almost immediately, she heard a series of three knocks coming from inside the square top wagon where she was sitting. She knew this was her sign and, for the first evening in many, slept soundly that night. These three knocks would happen at the same time every evening for the next three years until my mother had, albeit briefly, recovered her mental well-being.

I thought about this story as I entered the theatre and paid a few pounds for the attendance fee. Barton Street Theatre was an old-fashioned building with a good-sized stage, and the auditorium was full of people who all waited hopefully for a message from their deceased loved ones. Interested but not expectant, I chose to sit at the back near the exit. The psychic took centre stage, greeted the audience, and exclaimed that he had recently come out of hospital after suffering a short illness and wasn't up to giving messages that evening. Many audience members visibly showed their disappointment, with their shoulders slumping, heads turning, and much muttering, before the psychic stated that he had invited Anne, a guest medium from the north of England who would give the readings that night.

The audience's interest was piqued again as Mike Dee introduced the woman onto the stage. It was immediately clear to me and a few others in the room that she was struggling to make connections. My heart sank as I watched, thinking to myself that I had made a mistake in attending. I wondered if I should leave straight away, but I was concerned that my early exit would be noticed and commented on.

After a difficult first session, the audience filtered out into the bar to purchase their halftime drinks and exchange views on the woman who purported to be a psychic. Most people appeared to be disheartened. I spoke quietly to a couple who were standing to one side of the room and asked, "Is it always like this?" They both shook their heads and replied that the usual host was excellent but that this woman was clearly having a bad night. I speculated again internally about whether I should leave there and then, but something in the back of my mind suggested strongly that I should stay for the second half. Re-entering the auditorium, I sat at the back of the theatre next to the exit, thinking that I could slip out unnoticed if it was as unsatisfying as before. I figured I didn't need to worry about my possible early exit being inconspicuous, as I did not intend to return.

During one of the readings, my mobile phone rang as the woman on stage appeared to be having a particularly difficult time. I quickly turned it off, glancing up to see a few people staring disapprovingly at me. Still, I also observed that the usual psychic, who was seated at the back of the stage, was watching me with what appeared to be curiosity. The woman carried on attempting to make connections in a forced and somewhat desperate way when suddenly Mike Dee rose from his chair and said, "I'm going to have to stop you there, Anne, because I really need to speak with the man sat at the back of the room." He stepped down from the stage and greeted me with his hand outstretched. The heads of the audience were now turning to look at me, and an inner voice that sounded distinctly different from my own yet was somehow recognisable insisted, 'Don't speak, just listen'.

The medium took my hand in his and shook it vigorously, saying, "I've got to shake your hand; you are being congratulated for coming here tonight." He went on without pause, "When you came in, you arrived with two people, a man wearing a blue suit and a trilby hat, who has always been with you and will always be by your side, and a woman who passed more recently and is waving at you like this." He then demonstrated the wave: holding his hand in front of and close to his chest and moving it back and forth in a short, frantic way, his palm almost a blur. I knew without question that he was referring to Zania, a friend and former band member who had passed a couple of years earlier. Again, the voice in my head reiterated that I should not speak; I should only listen.

Mike Dee took a step back and then continued, "They are telling me that you have been going through a difficult time, and it's all to do with an older male relative's money; they say you have been walking around with your head held down, but that you should be looking up. They want you to know that you did the right thing and that you are not responsible for the situation that has been caused within your family." I said nothing, giving no verbal indication of whether this was correct or not, yet realising that he was talking about the fact that a year earlier, I had discovered that an elderly unmarried uncle had (allegedly) been swindled out of fifty thousand pounds by a relation who claimed to be caring for him. I had blown the whistle about this, causing a major rift within the family, which had not yet healed.

He went on: "They are saying that had you not told your family about what was happening, your uncle would have been left with nothing, and the guilty person would have gone on to do the same to other vulnerable family members." He gazed at me intently then said, "They are telling me that you are currently surrounded by jealousy, in both your professional and personal life, but that you should not let this concern you. Continue to live your truth, and you will always rise to the top. Let your inner light shine, and your glow will attract the right people, at the right times, to further your life's purpose." He then paused, cocking his head as if listening, before continuing, "They are telling me that you have a gift, and that you have used this gift in all of your previous lives, but that for some reason you are choosing not to in this one. They want you to know that you can change this situation anytime and begin using the gifts you have always had throughout your many lifetimes. You should be shining brightly, as you were always intended to do." He took another step back, "I think they are done with you for now."

Without further ado, he began to walk back to the stage before halting, turning around, and quickly returning to me. My mind was racing, but still, a note of doubt tumbled through me. He stood before me and stared deeply into my eyes before stating, "They won't let me leave without saying these exact words to you." After steadying himself for a moment, he spoke clearly and deliberately. "They want you to know that the answer to all questions is you."

I immediately felt as if I'd been punched in the stomach, and the air in my body appeared to dissipate, and I gasped in amazement. He smiled, then turned and walked back towards the stage. All eyes in the room were still on me, and I, dumbfounded, my thoughts whirling, watched as he took his seat, indicating that Anne should now continue with her readings.

As I left the theatre and drove home, memories of my childhood's many psychic events flooded through my mind, and I realised that an incredibly important life event had just occurred.

Chapter Twenty Nine

Ridicule, Resentment, and Reassurance

There is a short period in the summer months between light and twilight when the birds have flown to their roosts, and the skies become still, that I absolutely love. The daylight has disappeared, yet it's still far from full dark. Dusk doesn't last long, even in summertime, maybe fifteen minutes, but it's a magical spell. I like to sit outside in warm weather and experience the stillness, and it's during these moments that thoughts sometimes come to me that are not necessarily my own. I like to think that becoming one with the universe feels like this. I meditate on the mysteries of life and fancy that I can tap into a universal knowledge available to all of us if we know how to listen.

    I use moments like this to make my most important decisions. I find that quiet and tranquillity help me with my choices, and my judgment appears sharper and more intuitive. Suppose I've spent the day worrying about an issue, going back and forth in my mind, unsure of what to do or whether to do anything at all. In that case, this short span of time brings a cessation of any turmoil I might be feeling, and a calmness envelopes me before the answers to the questions I've been wrestling with appear fully formed in my mind. I know better than to question further when this happens; I am simply grateful that the unseen world has reached out to help me.

Following the reintroduction of the man in the blue suit's presence in my life in my mid-thirties, events started to move at a faster pace. The rate of paranormal (if that's the right word) occurrences increased exponentially. Occasionally, I was perturbed or scared by these incidents, but please understand that I was never harmed in any way by any of these episodes.

One evening, when I was in bed just drifting off to sleep, I was intensely aware that a presence had entered my bedroom. I was feeling pretty low at the time as I was having a difficult time at work, mainly due to the resentment of my success from colleagues who, just as the psychic Mike Dee had said on that fateful night in Barton Street Theatre, surrounded me with jealousy. It's my experience that, when people think evil thoughts about a person in a targeted and directive manner, this can have a very real physical effect on the person these toxic thought forms are directed at. Some Romany people believe that this is how curses work. Intentions can be highly potent, especially if the person the thoughts are intended for doesn't understand how to protect themselves psychically.

I recall sitting up in bed on this first occasion with my arm outstretched and my hand blocking the presence from entering further into the room, saying, "No, no, no, I don't want this." The presence immediately left. I sat up in bed, feeling a little unnerved but also perplexed as, when I thought about it, I couldn't understand why I was unsettled and disconcerted. I eventually reasoned that it was because it was so unexpected. I lay back down, thinking that if this experience ever happened again, I would let it play out.

Several nights later, I had the opportunity to do just that. Once again, it had been a difficult day at work. I was now more willing to speak openly about my beliefs, but this often came with ridicule and scepticism from some people, who tried to use my beliefs to undermine my professionalism. I had filmed, edited, and produced a video that promoted the innovative work we were doing with people with learning disabilities for the local authority. This was being shown at a major event that included influential people from the authority, parents and carers, and people from 'The King's Fund' who would be reporting on our achievements directly to the government of the time.

During the drinks and refreshments after the screening, which had gone extremely well, an influential member of the King's Fund group approached me with a senior council official to congratulate me on the video. One of my colleagues, who was particularly resentful of my success, stood nearby listening intently. He couldn't resist butting in and saying, in a pseudo-joking way intended to embarrass and sabotage my achievement, "You know that he believes in aliens though, don't you? I'm surprised he didn't have UFOs featured in the video."

The woman from the King's Fund and the male councillor looked at me questioningly, and I said as lightly as I could, "Well, you'd have to be a pretty arrogant person to think that we are the most intelligent beings in this vast universe."

They both gazed intently at me for a moment. Then the woman, giving my colleague a quick sideways glance before turning away from him and giving me her full attention, said, "Yes, you're absolutely right; it would be arrogant and extremely short-sighted to think that. The world could do with more open-minded people like you." We carried on chatting for some time in a warm and friendly manner that infuriated my now crestfallen colleague, who, being ignored, slunk quickly out of sight and left the party unnoticed.

That night, as I lay in bed thinking about what had happened earlier, I was still feeling wound up and a little stressed, and it took quite a while for me to drift off to sleep. I was in that state of awareness where you're not asleep but also not fully awake, still aware of what's happening around you, but with part of your consciousness somewhere else.

Suddenly, I felt a presence enter my bedroom. I was now fully awake but kept my eyes tightly shut. I felt the presence that I somehow knew was male, walk around to the side of my bed, pause for a moment, and then sit on the bed. As this happened, I felt the mattress depress, as if the being had physical weight. There was another pause, though it seemed like a long time, and I was just about to freak out when the presence lay beside me and wrapped his arms around me. This act filled me with a warm, comforting glow and the knowledge and total belief that everything would be alright. I instantly experienced a sense of reassurance and love, as if my heart, indeed my whole being, had been filled with warm golden light. I fell asleep a few seconds later and slept soundly for the first time in weeks.

When I awoke the next morning, I felt as if a weight had been lifted from me, and I knew in my soul that I was being taken care of. Answers to questions I hadn't even asked yet would appear when the time was right. All I needed was faith that the unseen forces were working in my favour. Although that faith has been stretched on many occasions, like a steel bed spring, it has always, so far, pinged back without breaking.

Chapter Thirty
The Twelve Apostles

When I was a teenager, I happened across a picture of the Twelve Apostles, a series of rock stacks on a beach near Port Campbell, next to the Great Ocean Road in Victoria, Australia. For some reason, the picture resonated powerfully with me. I felt as if I'd seen them before and had a mental image of walking with someone along the beach, looking up at the grandeur of the formations rising out of the waves.

I liked all things Australian, especially the Aussie films shown as a season on BBC2. We used to have end-of-term film showings at Canon Frome School, one of which was 'Walkabout'. I have watched this film many times since and have never tired of its magnificent beauty. I begged Mam for a poster of the Twelve Apostles, which she eventually bought for me. I recall saying that I would one day walk on that beach, which upset Mam as she never liked her children to be too far away. She would say, "Don't be divvy, that's the other side of the world!" The thought would not leave me, though.

I often felt that I didn't quite fit in anywhere, yet I craved acceptance. Many other Romany chavvies wanted nothing more than to be like their parents. I wanted, in fact, needed more. I knew working on the land or going out calling would never be enough for me. Although Romanies have a rich history, and family life is incredibly important, I knew there was another path for me, one that was less travelled and more difficult, and one that I knew I had no choice but to walk.

As a teen, I was expected to help with tasks like bale hauling during the summer holidays. This was hard, heavy work, but the payoff was riding on top of the unsteady load back to the farm before disembarking and loading the bales of straw into the barn. Most of the older local kids helped out with this, and we actually had a smoking den made of straw bales and used old hubcaps for ashtrays! Looking back, it's a miracle that we didn't burn the barn down with us inside it. The possible dangers never crossed our minds, though, probably because you think disaster will never strike when you're young. Apart from the health and safety aspects, this rarely happens today because very few farmers still use traditional oblong bales, instead rolling the straw into giant circular ones.

Things have changed considerably in the Romany Gypsy and Irish Traveller communities over the past forty or fifty years. Traditional stopping places have disappeared, as have many historically significant work roles that played a large part in our community's earning possibilities. We no longer comprise the bulk of the seasonal workforce many farmers once relied upon.

Romany Gypsies have been forced by the push of persecution and the pull of needing to earn a living into a variety of other professions. As more children leave school with an education, we have moved into a myriad of different positions. I initially thought about working as a journalist as I'd always enjoyed writing, but I was deterred from doing this by what I thought of as limitations due to my ethnicity. I had not heard of any Gypsy journalists in the 1970s. As far as I was aware, there were no peers in this profession that I could look up to.

When I spoke about this ambition to other Romanies, including my own family, it was generally frowned upon and derided, with people saying things like "We will never be accepted in jobs like that". It doesn't take much when you're a teenager to be dissuaded from following your heart. I read voraciously and appreciated literature. Reading took me to other places and worlds that I believed were infinitely more interesting and exciting than my own. As much as I relished village and country life, I ached for something I didn't think I could have: fulfilment and recognition for being good at something that made a difference to me and others.

I never minded being alone and following my own path. I've always enjoyed the company of others, but mostly on my own terms. As long as I had music and books, I could amuse myself, and as a teen, pretty much all of my pocket money and any earnings from fruit picking was spent on these items. Even today, one of my greatest joys is searching through the racks in a record store. After leaving school in 1977, having gained five top grades, I worked my way through various jobs, including farming, factory, and shop roles, until I eventually moved into care work in the late 1980s as a residential social worker. For the first time, I had found a post that inspired me. In 1993, I successfully applied for a position with the local authority and moved to Ross-on-Wye.

When certain friends entered my life, I sensed that I had always known them. It was like that with Les, my song-writing partner, and so it was with Alison Fletcher. When she walked into the day centre on her first morning on the job in 1994, we just looked at each other and laughed. I recall thinking, 'Where have you been all this time?' I am convinced that these individuals are part of my soul group and that we have lived many lives together.

I felt completely comfortable with Alison, and she was the first person at work that I came out to about my sexuality. I had already disclosed this to my parents after meeting my first boyfriend in the mid-1980s. My father was brilliant when I told him I was gay. He said he had always known and that it was no one's business but my own. Mam took it harder, probably because she was worried about how difficult this could make my life, but she told me she would always love me, no matter what happened. Mam said, "You've got a good heart, my boy, and the Lord will always look after you", and so far, she's been right.

Looking back, it's clear that my family had known since I was quite young. They just chose not to discuss the matter, and apart from a few people, still don't to this day. This is something I can live with because of how few of us actually discuss sexuality of any kind in the Romany community. Hopefully though, this is now beginning to change.

I've been incredibly lucky with my choice of friends. Alison's family has always treated me as one of their own. They live their lives without prejudice or hate and have supported me through some difficult times. Jamie, Ali's husband, had spent time in Sydney, Australia, and often spoke about his experience, saying he had loved his time there and encouraged me to visit the continent.

A few years later, the centre manager mentioned during a morning briefing that he would support any member of staff who wanted to job swop and gain experience at another day service. I left the meeting wondering how far I could take this. Later that day, I walked into the manager's office and said, "I want to go to Australia." Den Humble didn't even blink. He simply said, "Set it up then."

The career exchange with a woman called Marlene happened in January 1997. I received job offers from every state in Australia, but I was drawn to Geelong in Victoria. Geelong is a forty-minute drive from Melbourne, nestled in Corio Bay. The second biggest port city in Victoria, it is known worldwide for its wool production and is the gateway to the Great Ocean Road. Alison's Sister Kathy flew with me to help me settle in for the first three months, and as soon as we exited Tullamarine airport in Melbourne, I had the feeling of coming home. This sense of déjà vu followed me wherever I went. I had no trouble finding my way about the area, and Kathy couldn't understand how I appeared to know in advance what was around the next corner when we were out driving and sightseeing.

I revelled in my post at Coriolong Community Programmes, loving everything about the job and Australia. Three weeks after arriving, I met Andrew. I had been running a relationship and sexuality course from a room above the courthouse café, and at the end of the session, I walked through Johnstone Park and saw Andrew sitting on a bench eating his lunch. We hit it off immediately, and again, I had the familiar feeling of always having known him, and he felt the same.

We moved in together within a month and everything just clicked. There was no doubt in either of our minds that it was the right thing to do. Andrew only came out to his family after meeting me; his father had died some years before, but the night he introduced me to his mother is now etched upon my memory. Many of Andrew's family lived in Corio, one of the poorer parts of the city, and the venues there were traditional Aussie Inns. The people frequenting them were hard-working and knew how to handle themselves, including the women.

When we walked into the packed pub, Nancy, Andrew's mum, rose from her seat and walked straight up to where we stood in the middle of the bar. She looked me up and down slowly before roaring, with a voice that sounded like a box of rusty nails, "So Andrew, this is your gay lover, is it!" Everything in the room stilled and went deadly quiet. I thought my heart would stop and wanted the floor to open up beneath me before Nancy thundered, "Anyone who's got a problem with them will have to go through me first." She glared around the room defiantly. No one moved or said a word, and gradually, the hubbub rose again as usual.

Nancy always welcomed us in her home, and we never left without food from her freezer. Andrew comes from a large family who all accepted us, especially his aunt and uncle, Bubby and Neil, whom we visited often. We had a wonderful year before the time came, all too quickly, due to my work visa ending, for me to return home.

Andrew arrived in the UK a month after I had returned. He could only get a six-month holiday visa, but we had a great time. He met my family and friends, and I was able to take some time off work to show him the country. Mam and Dad got on fine with Andrew, and he thought the world of them. He was genuinely touched when they bought us both Christmas presents.

We wanted to stay together but needed to prove to the authorities that we had lived in a relationship for two years to qualify him to move here. This was at a time before civil partnerships or marriage for gay people existed. Andrew moving to the UK was our best option as my parents were elderly and needed more support. My brother and sister were married, so Mam and Dad's care was left to me. I don't regret being in this position and have no sense of resentment towards my parents, who have now both passed over some years ago. They gave their all to me, and it was only fitting that I did the same for them.

When the six months were up, Andrew had to leave the UK due to his visa restrictions, but six weeks after going home, he attempted to enter the country again for a further six months; this would enable us to meet the two-year requirement needed for him to apply to stay permanently. I was at Heathrow Airport to meet him, excited to be seeing him again. I waited impatiently and watched anxiously for him to appear through checkout. When he didn't, I knew something was wrong.

Abruptly, an announcement came over the tannoy system asking me to go to the immigration section. When I saw how distraught Andrew was, my fears were confirmed. We were led into a room, where I noticed the table and chairs were bolted to the floor. The immigration officer said he believed Andrew was entering the country with no intention of leaving after six months. We admitted that was indeed the plan and explained our situation. The officer stated that Andrew must return to Australia on the next available flight and apply from his own country. We tried to explain that this meant we would never be able to meet the two-year requirement, but he appeared uninterested in our predicament. I then realised why the table and chairs were bolted to the floor: I certainly wanted to throw them around the room. After virtually begging, we managed to get the officer to agree to Andrew staying for one week, after which he would be forced to leave the country.

I contacted my MP and various agencies, none of whom could change the situation or even offered to help. When I took Andrew to the airport at the end of an emotional week, it was one of the worst days of our lives. I saw Andrew again when I returned to Australia at the end of 1999 to see in the millennium with him in Geelong. It was as if we'd never been apart when we were together, but we only had a month. We returned to the Twelve Apostles and walked on the beach again, just as I'd seen in my mind when I was a teenager.

Some people like to differentiate between what they see as different kinds of love. Gay love, straight love, familial love, or love between friends, and even pets and animals. I don't make those distinctions. Love is love. Even when it breaks your heart, it's still the only thing that's real or worth having. It's been many years since Andrew and I have seen each other, although we still speak by telephone regularly and will continue to do so until the day comes (God Willing) when we meet again.

Chapter Thirty One
Ravens and Revelations

Some things take a long time to connect, sometimes weeks, years, or even decades. I remember walking with my mother through a shaded wood to a Black and White cottage in the late summer of 1970 when I was nine years old. The house was owned by an elderly man, who to me resembled the wizard 'Cadelin' from a book that I had recently read for the first time called 'The Weirdstone of Brisingamen'. The 'wizard's' house was also a repair shop, and the owner specialised in repairing jewellery, watches, and some sundry household items.

The early 70s was a time when objects and belongings were not thrown away when they stopped working or broke; wherever possible, things were repaired. These days, some people will order clothing online or buy something from a clothes store and wear it once, and then often it is discarded or passed on to a charity shop, where it's sometimes sold for more than the original store price! In the 1970s, people simply didn't have the money to do this. We were taught to look after our clothes as often they would be handed down to younger siblings. I was lucky to have an older brother who was fashion-conscious and sartorially aware, so I always had a supply of nice clothing coming down the line.

As my mother and I entered the shop, the familiar sound of a bell jingled, as this was the greeting in most stores at the time. Independent stores were plentiful then, giving, I believe, far more variety and choice than the current high streets or village stores. It didn't appear strange to me that the 'wizard's' shop and home were in a cottage in a wood, as this was commonplace at the time. Village stores and post offices were often run from people's homes. As we entered, I was surprised to see what the 'wizard' explained was a young raven nursing an injured leg in a large cage that hung from a chain in the corner of the shop front. The room was filled with many other curiosities, but the bird held my full attention. The juvenile raven's right leg was bandaged, and it held it off the sawdust-covered floor of the cage to avoid pain or further injury, I supposed.

The bird stared at me with calm and calculating eyes, its intelligence immediately evident. I stared back in wonder at its beauty and magnificence. I sensed straight away that this bird found me as fascinating as I found it. Mam and the wizard-come shopkeeper were chatting amiably, and Mam was enquiring how long the repair of the clasp on the gold charm bracelet she liked to wear would take.

When they finished their pleasantries, the elderly wizard/repair man informed Mam that her bracelet would be ready for collection in a week. The tall, white-haired man, sporting a full and well-kept long beard, came around from behind his shop counter. As he stood next to me, I noticed he was wearing a pair of baggy striped trousers held up by braces matched with a white linen shirt and a black waistcoat.

"I rescued this young raven several weeks ago," he said. "Since then, we've become quite good friends."

"Does he have a name?" I enquired.

"No," replied the wizard. "He will have recovered and be ready to be released back into the wild soon, so it didn't seem right to name him, as he is a wild bird and not a pet."

The 'wizard' explained that ravens lived for a long time, sometimes well over forty years and that they paired for life. "All Corvid's are intelligent," he said, "but ravens are the most intelligent of them all. Did you know that they can recognise people they have seen from years before and pass on information to other ravens about that person, such as whether they are kind and safe to be around or cruel and to be avoided?"

I admitted that I didn't know this and asked, "Will this raven remember me?"

"Oh, I'm sure he will," replied the 'wizard' in his beneficent manner. "He may tell other ravens that you are a kind boy, and who knows…?" He gazed thoughtfully at me and then at the bird before saying, "You might get the chance to rescue a raven, or some other creature yourself one day."

Mam stood on the other side of me and took my hand in hers. "It's time to go," she said. "You can see the bird again next week when we collect my bracelet". We bade the shopkeeper goodbye and left the shop, with the raven watching my every move in what appeared to be a contemplative way before croaking its goodbye as we stepped through the door.

Around 2018, when I was managing Travellers' Times, I was asked by a Chief Constable, as part of my role with West Mercia Police's IAG (Independent Advice Group), to train a group of largely experienced police officers from Herefordshire in Gypsy and Traveller awareness. I readily agreed to do this because my father had always told me that if I wanted to change something, the best way to do it was from the inside. People in positions of power, such as police officers, judges, MPs and local councillors, often have the greatest need for awareness training but not the self-awareness to know this.

Cognitive dissonance is a real issue for some of these people because they simply do not, or cannot, accept that Gypsies and Travellers experience racism and prejudice in the same way as Black or Asian people do. They cannot admit to themselves that we are legitimate ethnicities because that would mean that they would have to change how they treat us; their prejudice and bias are so ingrained within them that changing their thought patterns would take more effort than they are willing or able to expend.

I was well prepared when I arrived at Hereford Police Station on the day in question. I had put together a training package that included the key histories of Gypsies and Travellers in Britain and Europe, including also the Northern Indian heritage of Romany Gypsies and the Western heritage of Irish Travellers as indigenous to Ireland. The training would also explain the critical cultural differences between our ethnicities. Along with this, I gave facts and figures about the frequency and types of racism and prejudice that we experience, that I had gleaned from some of the Non-Government Organisations such as 'Friends, Families, and Travellers' and 'The Traveller Movement', and I provided recommendations as to how services such as the police could more successfully engage with the Gypsy and Traveller communities.

The Chief Constable accompanied me into a large room with more people than I expected. There were at least forty officers in the room, which surprised me as I'd been told it would probably be around 15-20 people. The Chief's introduction explained my role within the IAG and gave some background information about me, including that I had managed several Learning Disability services for the local authority and my current role at Travellers' Times.

Most Romany Gypsies have a kind of superpower. We are adept at picking up micro-aggressions and hidden hostile attitudes. We've gained this power by experiencing racism and prejudice for the majority of our lives, and I sensed these attitudes in the air as soon as I entered the room. I and many other Romanies have learned not to react when we perceive these emotions because, if we did, we would be constantly arguing with people or defending ourselves from the negative stereotypes they hold. No one can live like that for extended periods without experiencing dire health consequences.

After the Chief Constable had completed my introduction, he left the room, and I settled into my seat before starting my presentation. Some officers in the room made eye contact with me and returned my smiles of greeting, others ignored me and carried on chatting, and some actively looked away when I made eye contact with them.

I began by thanking them for taking the time to be there and said I was grateful that the Chief had asked me to do the training and that I hoped it would lead to more positive engagement between the police service and Gypsies and Travellers. My words were received with nothing but a deafening silence. I carried on and was about a third of the way through my forty-minute presentation, speaking about some of the prejudice that our children regularly experience in schools and how services like the NHS often discriminate unfairly against Gypsies and Travellers when we see doctors or attend hospitals for treatment. Without warning, a male officer at the back of the room stood up and proclaimed loudly that he had never met a Gypsy who wasn't a criminal.

I was acutely aware that every eye in the room was on me and expectantly waiting for my response to this unexpected statement. I paused and looked around the room, allowing time for someone to disagree with the officer, who still stood, staring at me with a satisfied smirk. No one did. Not even the one officer in the room I had met previously, and whom I knew was of Irish Traveller heritage.

I paused and collected myself for a moment before looking at the officer who had made the offensive statement and saying, "Well, you have met one now, cos' I'm sat right here in front of you, mate." Then I continued, "Have you ever considered that Gypsies and Travellers work in all kinds of professions, such as shop workers, nurses, managers, the armed forces or even the police service?" The officer of Irish Traveller heritage shifted uncomfortably in his seat when I said this, but still, he said nothing. I looked again around the room. "How many people here think it would have been acceptable to make a statement like that to a Black or Asian person?" I ventured. This question, too, was met with silence, although by now, many officers in the room were looking distinctly uncomfortable, because they knew that their bias and prejudice had been exposed. "Perhaps this would be a good time to take a comfort break," I said, standing up to let people know that this part of the session was over.

The revelation came to me that either every other officer in that room believed the same thing that the police officer who had made the statement did, or the offending officer was simply a bully and the other officers were intimidated into silence/agreement, which was possibly the case for the officer of Irish Traveller heritage. It could have been a combination of both scenarios neither of which was acceptable to me or should have been acceptable to them.

I hadn't reckoned on the events of that training session having such a profound effect on me. But they did. Romany Gypsies have been reviled since we first appeared in this country over six hundred years ago. Still, the comments and attitudes in that room at Hereford police station resonated unpleasantly with me; so raw was the wound inflicted on me by the police officer's words and the attitudes of the others present, that I did not agree to provide further training for nearly a year. I needed time to regain my equilibrium and develop a better strategy for future training events.

Eventually, when I agreed to provide training for West Mercia and Warwickshire police again, I knew I would have to change my approach. I had been booked for a training session at Hindlip, West Mercia's Headquarters, as part of my Independent Advisory role, along with other trainers who spoke about disabilities and LGBTQ+ issues. I was the last to speak, and the previous speakers took their place at the back of the room to listen along with the mainly new police officer recruits. This time, I had decided to mostly forego the facts and figures that I had formerly used and instead concentrated on my own and my family's experience of racism and prejudice. I made it personal for the people listening and personal for me.

I shared experiences that were difficult for me to speak about, including how these experiences had affected my mental health, my sense of self-worth, and my outlook on life. When I finished, there was a moment of silence before the whole audience rose to their feet and applauded. The applause was sustained for several minutes, and I was shocked and relieved that this was their reaction. This had never happened in any of my previous training sessions. However, my change of tack had helped the people present to empathise with me and to better understand the experiences of Gypsies and Travellers. I learned a big lesson that day; you have to give of yourself to reach people and change their preconceptions.

Over the years, I have provided Gypsy and Traveller Awareness training for various healthcare and care services and the police and CPS (Crime Prosecution Service) on numerous occasions. Some of my talks and sessions are on YouTube and various other websites, including a lecture I did for West Mercia Police's 'Race Hate Awareness' week in 2024. This occurred in front of many senior officers and people in positions of power and authority from the CPS and the West Midlands Crime Commissioners Office.

I have gained a reputation for not 'sugaring the pill' when it comes to providing awareness training. I'm not afraid to use examples from mine or my family's experience, and I call out racism and prejudice wherever I see it. I've seen and experienced a lot of it when providing training, which in itself shows just how much cognitive dissonance is out there when it comes to challenging the stereotypes, prejudices, and biases people hold about Gypsies and Travellers.

The people in positions of power who perpetuate these negative opinions of Gypsies and Travellers need to be held to account, not just by Gypsies and Travellers, but by gorjas too. Just as Black and Asian people needed other ethnicities to champion their cause, so do we, and this extends to companies and organisations. I have worked for and with many care organisations, for example, and have mentioned that I provide Gypsy and Traveller awareness training only to be met with the response, "Well, we don't have any of those people here, so there's no need to provide this training." I've often had to point out that not only am I a Romany Gypsy, but that I'm fully aware that there are other staff members or service users who are as well. It's just that the companies involved have not provided a safe space for Gypsies and Travellers to be able to disclose their ethnicity.

The lack of organisational awareness of their duties under the Equality Act is sometimes quite astounding. Organisations often believe that because there is a written 'equality' policy in place, then that is all they need to provide. Nothing could be further from the truth. Face-to-face training from people with lived experience is extremely important, and at the very least, online training should be provided.

In 2023 I was invited by The University of Worcester to be part of the team who put together the first mandatory online training package in Gypsy and Traveller Awareness for social workers for Worcestershire Council. Other authorities have since adopted this, and it's vital that professional people acquire this training to ensure that Gypsies and Travellers can have confidence that prejudice and bias towards them will not be apparent when accessing services.

All too often Gypsies and Travellers have been ill-served by services that are meant to be protecting us or providing us with health care. Many Gypsies and Travellers deliberately deny their heritage due to the fear of receiving poor service, and this is especially true when receiving health care. The fear of this is so great for some people that they put off going to see a doctor for as long as possible, and this alone probably accounts for the fact that our life expectancy is 10-20 years shorter than the average person in Great Britain, including when compared with other ethnicities.

In 2015, probably because I had spent forty years smoking cigarettes, and partly I believe because of the pressures of working in management for my local authority, I suffered a heart attack. I took my role as a day services manager seriously. I strived to provide systems of care that encouraged people to have fundamental, fulfilling roles within their communities, where they are valued for their contributions. I also encouraged staff to be innovative and gave them the tools they needed to improve their performance and move on to better positions. I've worked with some managers who deny their staff training to keep them in their roles or, more precisely, in their place. This approach never works because good and competent people will always find a way to move on. Managers who help people to do this will at least have a reputation for fairness and altruism. This approach is infinitely better than the alternative, one of meanness and self-interest that some managers I've known have been left with.

Although I quickly recovered from my heart issue after having a couple of stents fitted, it meant that when COVID-19 hit our shores in 2020, I was advised by my doctor to shield myself away from people. I worked for a care organisation then and had to inform them I would need to take some time away until the much-trumpeted vaccine had been rolled out.

I've always been comfortable with my own company, but during that year, I struggled with loneliness, which was why I decided to rescue and home a dog. Having 'Mr. Pickle', a handsome Jack Russell to look after, was good for me and ensured that I took full advantage of the hour or so we could go out in public each day, as he required regular walks. I liked to take him to quiet spots in the countryside where I could let him off lead, and he could run till his heart was content. One of my favourite places was at Yarkhill, where I had grown up, and I relished the open spaces, and the fields and the streams of my youth that I knew so well. It is still a cherished place for me.

One afternoon, as we exited a wooded area where Pickle had enjoyed the sights, sounds, and smells immensely, we entered a large open field with a tumbledown unused cowshed at one end and a brook at the other. On the other side of the field, near the cowshed, I noticed what appeared to be large round metal wire containers on the ground. Intrigued, I snapped the lead onto Pickle's harness and set off across the field. As we got closer, I could see that there were birds inside the cages. Upon closer inspection, I could see that these cages were traps and were of the maze type, where once an animal had gone in, there was no way for them to get out. There were two magpies in one trap, and in the other, a large raven watched me and Pickle warily. I couldn't bear the thought of these birds starving to death or dying of dehydration, and I realised that I would have to set them free. With some difficulty, I managed to open the cage containing the magpies first. They exited quickly and flew away without as much as a backward glance.

I then turned my attention to the other cage, where the sizeable elderly-looking raven eyed me with what seemed to me to be expectation and interest. The raven's cage was larger and more challenging to get into, and I had to spend a few minutes working out how best to get the bird out of the trap. All the while, the bird regarded me and seemed intrigued by my actions. When I finally opened the last trapdoor, the raven paused, and then casually walked out of the cage onto the grass. It stood for a moment looking at me and Mr Pickle, whose lead I kept a tight grip on, even though my dog did not move towards the sizeable bird; the raven then stretched its wings to its full and impressive wingspan and lifted off the ground almost in slow motion.

It descended onto a post about twenty feet away and turned its body to look at me. The bird observed me for a few minutes as I walked away with my dog by my side before suddenly giving a loud croak and flying away. When I heard the croak, the memory of the 'wizard's' words tumbled into my mind. I cannot, of course, say that it was the same raven that had held me enthralled on that summer's day in 1970, but nor can I say for sure that it wasn't.

Chapter Thirty Two
Otherworldly Observations

In 1972 Noele Gordon was a massive television star. She played Meg Mortimer, and later, the character was known even more famously as Meg Richardson, the owner and matriarch of the fictional Crossroads Motel. Crossroads was a teatime soap opera famous for its shaky sets and outrageous storylines (later, brilliantly spoofed by Victoria Wood as 'Acorn Antiques'). The programme started in the 1960s and ended in the 1980s. Noele Gordon was with the show for almost its entire run and was the only cast member who had a full-time contract with ATV, which made the series.

She lived near Ross-on-Wye, in a large, rambling property just off the A40, called Weir End House. She was a popular figure in the local area and could often be seen out and about, walking or shopping. On a Saturday morning, when I was eleven years old and accompanying my mother while she did the weekly shop in Hereford, we spotted a long line of people queuing to get a signed photograph of Noele, who was sat behind a table opposite the entrance to the Butter Market, signing pictures of herself and chatting briefly with each person in turn.

Crossroads was Mam's favourite programme, and we eagerly joined the queue and waited patiently for our turn. When it eventually came, Mam, feeling a little star-struck, pushed me forward to ask for the autograph. Noele Gordon raised her head and looked at me steadily for a moment before saying, "Ah, a youthful fan, and what's your name, young man?" I told her, and she continued, "And who's your favourite character in Crossroads?" I looked quizzically at her, unsure what she meant, "Who do you like best in the show?" she clarified.

My empathic abilities were well attuned even at my young age, and I knew what she needed to hear. "Oh, you are, Meg", I replied. "Mam likes you best too, don't you, Mam?" I looked at my mother, who was shyly beaming her lovely smile.

Whilst signing a photograph of her that had been taken at least twenty years earlier, Noele said, "You've got a very polite boy there; he's a credit to you." Mam bristled with pride but appeared dumbstruck. Noele Gordon looked again at me over her large square-framed glasses and said, "I'm sure we'll meet again one day, young man." Then we were moved on by the person organising the signing, and another fan stood before Noele, waiting for their name to be asked.

Almost twenty-five years later, I was employed at The Ryefield Centre in Ross-on-Wye and was doing outreach work with some service users who lived at Weir End House. The property had been turned into a residential home for people with learning difficulties after Noele (the former owner) passed over in the late 1980s and had been buried in St Mary's churchyard in Ross. The work at Weir End allowed me to explore the house and gardens where the Crossroads star had lived.

On a warm, sunny, early autumn day, I sat in the extensive garden alongside one of the service users, Joan, eating my lunch. I liked Joan, who had a lovely, sensitive personality and a great sense of humour. We were chatting amiably when suddenly I saw Noele Gordon appear through the sunbeams and walk towards us as we sat on the metal bench. She wore a floral two-piece suit and white shoes and looked like I remembered her in Crossroads. The apparition paused as it passed where we sat and, glancing at me, said, "I told you we'd meet again."

She then smiled warmly and carried on walking, disappearing before she reached the bottom of the garden.

Amazed, I looked at Joan, who was smiling broadly. Joan said, "She's gone now."

"Have you seen her before, Joan?" I asked.

Joan nodded and said, as if nothing was out of the ordinary, "Noele Gordon, she used to live here."

To make music in a band, you must collaborate and, to some extent, be willing to lose your ego. Although this sounds simple, it really isn't, and clashing egos are often the main reason bands break up. Les Scarrott (Lez Shed) and I collaborated successfully for nearly thirty years. We have released five albums of our music over this period. We are not prolific writers, but music has been a consistent factor in our long friendship. We have similar backgrounds and, in many ways, a shared outlook on life. There have been occasions when the band has been on the back burner in our lives, such as when I lived and worked in Australia for a year or when Les was busy bringing up his son, but we always knew that we would make music again at some point.

When I returned from my sojourn in Australia in 1997, we were eager to make more music together. We began gigging again in earnest and enjoyed performing in front of an audience, but writing, producing, and recording our songs was our first love. The central core of the Brickshed has always been me and Les, as songwriters and singers, but we have welcomed a wide selection of people to join us over the years to enhance our sound and bring fresh ideas. In 2001, we embarked on the making of 'Corn Circles', one of our most successful albums and one that we are particularly proud of.

I was designing the cover for the album on 9/11/2001, using my recently purchased first computer, a blueberry-coloured Apple iMac that had opened up a whole new world of possibilities for us as a band. The television in my bedroom was on at the same time, and I became aware that something enormous was happening when the first reports about the terror attacks began appearing on the screen. As I viewed the scene, I could see that the first plane had already hit one of the twin towers in New York. I then watched in horror as the second plane hit the other tower in real-time, live on TV. Whilst staring open-mouthed at the screen, I witnessed the plane strike the tower and disappear inside the structure.

I immediately picked up my phone and called Les, urging him to turn his TV on. When he did, neither of us could believe what we were witnessing. Many strange things happened that day, including the collapse of a third building, supposedly caused by a fire in the lobby. However, this has never sat well with me, and I remain unconvinced by the official explanations, as are many others.

Following the release of the 'Corn Circles' album, Les and I decided to invite some other people to join the band so that, when we performed live, we could have a bigger sound, one that was more faithful to the music we had created on our albums. While rehearsing with the new members, orbs began showing up in our photographs.

After rehearsals, we often congregated at our friend Pam's house. Pam had suffered a stroke some years earlier: she was on her way home from the hospital after having a birthmark on her face removed when the stroke struck. The two incidents may have been unrelated, but Pam was convinced there was a link. Her son, Ciaran, was now our drummer, and we often met up at the house he shared with his mother to relax following rehearsals. Pam's illness had left her with some paralysis on her left side and an Eastern European accent. This phenomenon has been reported by quite a number of people who have had injuries to their brains. The accent gave Pam a strange, exotic mystery that said, 'Here is someone who has lived a life'. Pam played up to this impression to the full. She enjoyed that people thought she knew more, especially spiritually, than they did.

One evening, while we were drinking and chatting about all manner of things, spiritual and otherwise, I mentioned that I had recently read about photographic 'orbs of light' on the internet. Pam was immediately intrigued, and a discussion regarding what these orbs might be ensued. While we talked and tossed around different theories, I remembered that I had a cheap 35mm disposable camera in my pocket, with only half of the film used. I had bought it when Mam and I had visited Aunt Mimey in the hospital in Evesham a few days earlier. I threw the camera to one of the other people present, saying, "Let's see if we have any orbs here." We began snapping pictures, each of us 'posing' with imaginary orbs and continuing the conversation about whether or not this was a natural phenomenon. We snapped pictures until the film was used up, and I said I would get the images developed before the next rehearsal.

A few days later, I handed the camera over to an assistant at a Boots chemist and asked for their one-hour service. Later, as I collected the pictures, the assistant remarked, "You've got a few ghosts on your prints." I looked at her quizzically, but she said no more, simply handing me the envelope containing the twenty-four pictures.

I opened the envelope as I walked down the stairs to the store's ground floor. I began flipping through the pictures quickly, thinking, 'See, no orb...' I stopped halfway down the stairs, staring at the picture in my hand. There I was posing with an orb in precisely the place I was pointing to in the shot. It was pretty big, pale silver, almost translucent, with concentric circles inside, which diminished in size as they got closer to the centre. I stared in disbelief before looking at the next shot; orbs were present on this one and the next too.

Orbs were on almost all of the shots taken at Pam's that night. I went through several possible explanations in my mind. Was it dust, refraction from the camera flash, or maybe a possibility I had yet to consider? My gut feeling said something else, though. My inner being screamed, 'You asked for proof, well this is it!' I turned around, walked back up the stairs and purchased another camera of the same kind. I showed the assistant (who had made the ghost remark) the pictures and asked her what she thought the objects were. Smiling, she shook her head, saying, "We see these things from time to time, but we can't say what they are."

The following week, after band practice, I handed the photos around, and another discussion ensued about what the objects could be. We used the whole film with the new camera, as everyone thought repeating the 'experiment' would be a good idea. A few days later, the film was developed, and the 'orbs' were in every picture this time. I took the prints to Les's flat. We laid them out on a large coffee table in his front room and began exchanging views about what the orbs could be and what was happening. We took turns playing devil's advocate, each of us searching for a rational explanation, and the one we kept coming back to was the dust in front of the lens theory. Paraphrasing the law of Occam's razor, we both felt this could not be discounted, as it was the simplest explanation.

It was while we were coming to this conclusion that we both looked up to the wall on our left because we had heard what sounded remarkably like the ringing of a ship's bell coming from it. The hairs on my neck stood to attention as I became aware of a scraping sound coming from the wall behind us. With my feet feeling like lead and rooted to the floor, Les and I turned our heads and upper bodies. We saw that the large wooden framed poster of Bob Dylan, which had hung in that spot since the day Les had moved in a couple of years earlier, was slowly swinging from side to side, the frame scraping against the painted wall as it did so. The poster began to swing faster as we beheld it before stopping suddenly. The paper print inside the glass-less frame rippled upwards, and the entire frame flipped off the nail which had secured the picture to the wall and landed on the floor with a clatter.

Things seemed to speed up then; we became aware of a rattling sound coming from a shelf on the wall to our right. We looked over in time to see a cassette tape from the back of the higgledy shelf fly up into the air and land on the floor in front of us, some six feet away from the wall where it had previously been. We then witnessed what appeared to be a grey, wispy, smoky entity shoot along the wall towards the bottom of the room, where a floor-standing hi-fi speaker stood with an indoor TV aerial placed upon it. The antenna began to vibrate at an incredibly fast rate until a screw that was lying on the sheepskin rug in the middle of the floor flew up into the air, hit the aerial, made it ping, and then everything stopped. It seemed as if all the air had been sucked out of the room, creating a silent vacuum.

Les broke the spell by bending down and picking up the cassette tape; he looked at it and then handed it to me. It was a compilation Les had made of Bob Dylan's gospel songs that he had entitled 'Gospel Bob'. I sat down on a nearby beanbag, holding the tape and shaking my head in wonder. It was as if something or someone was saying in my head, 'If you don't believe what's in the pictures, believe what you've just witnessed'. We didn't discuss further what had happened that evening. I think we were both in shock. I left shortly after, rerunning what had occurred in my mind, trying to make sense of it on the drive home. I didn't visit Les at his flat again for two weeks, although we met for band rehearsal as usual the following week and shared what we had witnessed, causing much discussion and a variety of theories to abound. Everyone agreed that although the event was shocking and a little scary, no harm had come to us during it. It was like a wake-up call or an affirmation that we were on the right path.

Dreams have always played a large part in my spiritual awakening. In the mid-1990s, I sang briefly with a band a friend had put together for a New Year's Eve gig called Mission Impossible. The seven-piece outfit went down well with audiences, and we created a big, warm sound, concentrating on cover versions that we knew the audiences would know and love. I was busy performing in two bands and appearing in theatre productions, all while working full-time.

On Thursday, the 13th of June 1996, I went to bed and had a vivid dream. When I awoke, I recalled the dream in every detail. I was so disturbed that when I arrived at work on the Friday morning, I couldn't wait to speak to my friend Alison about it. "I was in a pub in a large city," I explained. "All around me, I could see dust and rubble and bodies, I could hear people calling out for help, and a voice kept whispering in my ear: there's been a bomb blast, there's been a bomb blast." Alison knew from experience that my dreams were worth noting and, just as my Uncle Aldy had once stated, she said we should keep an eye on the news.

The morning of Saturday the 15th of June 1996, I was driving to Speech House in the Forest of Dean for a rehearsal with Mission Impossible. At approximately 11.30 am, a BBC announcement interrupted the radio show I was listening to, warning people to avoid central Manchester as an 'incident' had occurred. Immediately, I heard the voice whisper into my ear again, 'There's been a bomb blast, there's been a bomb blast'. I pulled over to the side of the road and sat quietly for a while, feeling completely helpless, as many who have these experiences do. I knew without doubt that the voice was correct and that my dream had indeed been a prophetic one.

Two hundred and twenty people were injured, some seriously, by the Manchester Pub Bombing. As the emergency services dealt with the wounded, the fire crews searched shops and offices for casualties. In the confusion, fallen shop mannequins were briefly mistaken for bodies. Many people were traumatised by the massive blast, which the IRA claimed responsibility for, but miraculously, no one was killed.

While recording the Corn Circles album in 2001, Les began having a strange reoccurring dream that happened for seven nights in a row. He reported that the dream seemed incredibly realistic and lucid, building in intensity each night. He relayed that, shortly after falling asleep, his dream would begin with several people appearing in his room and standing around his bed. They then talked with him about our music and the songs we wrote and recorded. Les asked if the songs would become well known, and they told him everyone knew and loved the songs in their dimension. Some of these beings wore what Les described as doctors' outfits, white jackets, or medical scrubs. During one of the later dreams, the entities asked if he wanted to see them in his dimension, but Les refused this offer as he was beginning to find the 'dreams' somewhat disturbing, especially as he would wake with a jolt when the dream ended. He found it very difficult to sleep again that night.

The dreams always ended the same way: Les would ask a series of questions about life, the universe, and how we could influence people to act for the betterment of the planet. The answer was always the same; he was told, in a tone he described as loving but urgent, 'The answer to all questions is you'.

Eighteen months later, I heard that statement again from the psychic Mike Dee on the night I went to Barton Street Theatre. It was the one single thing he said during my reading that convinced me absolutely that everything he had told me was true. Even I reasoned, if he was telepathic, how could he have plucked that phrase, which Les had repeated to me specifically, from my mind when I wasn't thinking about it then? The only thing that made sense to me was that this experience was not just real but a profound moment in my life. It was something I couldn't deny, a moment that changed my life forever.

Since that night in Gloucester, I have walked a different path that is not always clear or easy but is infinitely more rewarding and satisfying. It is a path that many others in the world have trod before and many more will tread in the future, but the one thing I know with certainty is that I don't walk alone. The man in the blue suit is always with me, and just as Mike Dee said, "Will always be with me."

He is my guide, a constant presence, here to look after me and comfort and support me through life's difficulties. I have known him since childhood, probably even before I incarnated onto this physical plain. He protects and loves me, and I'm grateful he is with me. I know that my spiritual work is only just beginning and that the Gypsy and Traveller awareness training I provide is just one part of it. I can only try to repay his love and support daily with loving actions and thoughts, and I will continue to do so until the day comes when he takes me by the hand and leads me home.

~~~The End~~~

Glossary – Romany Words

(Poggardi Jib to English Translation)

*Please note: spellings may differ in publications, as there are no definitive spellings of the Romany language. This is in no way an absolute list of all the words that are in common use.

Aitchin' Tan – Stopping Place
Bok – Luck (for example: Kushty Bok, Good Luck)
Calling – Hawking/selling items door to door
Chavvie – Child
Chavvies – Children
Chore – Steal
Chored – Stolen
Cosh – Stick
Couring – Fighting
Div – Fool
Divvy – Foolish
Dordy! – Well! (Example: Dordy, Dordy, Dordy! Well, Well, Well!)
Grois – Horses
Gorja/Gorger – Non-Gypsy or Traveller
Gavver – Police Officer
Jel Akie – Come Here
Jin – Know/Understand
Jucell – Dog
Kushty - Good
Knacker – Derogatory term for a Gypsy or Traveller
Luvver – Money
Mingeries – Police
Muskeror – Policeman
Mush/Moosh – Man
Mushes – Men

Mort – Woman (Usually an older woman)
Muller – Devil/Bad Spirit
Mullardi – Haunted
Mullered – Killed/Murdered
Needypek – Slur, not a real Gypsy or Traveller
Parnie – Water
Puv – Tether, (Example: Puv out the Grois, Tether the horses)
Poggardi Jib – Broken Language
Pogger/Poggering – Hit/Hitting
Rakli – Young Woman
Rummered – Married
Rutefull – Naughty
Tan – Home, or, The Place
Tuv – Cigarette
Torrati – Night/Tonight
Vonga – Money/Cash
Yog – Fire/Fireplace

Picture Glossary

Chapter One, Page 1
Elizabeth (Betty) Smith with her granddaughter,
Julie Haines at The Tan
1975, Yarkhill, Herefordshire.

Chapter Two, Page 9
Chris Smith, 1964, Yarkhill, Herefordshire.

Chapter Four, Page 14
Chris Smith, aged 9, 1970, Yarkhill, Herefordshire.

Chapter Five, Page 19
My mother, Elizabeth (Betty) Smith with her
best friend Doreen Scott
'Bine cutting' - Early 1970s, Yarkhill Herefordshire.

Chapter Six, Page 24
My father, Leonard Smith, with 'Old Silver'
1980s, Withington, Herefordshire.

Chapter Eight, Page 35
Chris Smith (Standing -far right) with 'The Cool Gang'
1975, Canon Frome Secondary School, Herefordshire.

Chapter Ten, Page 49
My paternal grandparents, Samuel and Ada Smith,
with my father, Leonard Smith on Granny's knee
1916, Forest of Dean, Gloucestershire.

Chapter Eleven, Page 55
My niece, Jenny Haines, in our shed,
Mid 1970s, Yarkhill, Herefordshire.

Chapter Thirteen, Page 69
Hop Pickers, Yarkhill Farm, Early 1970s.
Left to right- My uncle, Nelson Johns, Joey Johns,
Joannie Lee, Missy Johns, my aunt, Mimey Johns,
Mrs Boswell, Mr Boswell, Alice Evans, Betty Johns.

Chapter Fifteen, Page 78
Elizabeth (Betty) Smith, with 'Old Silver' and her dog, Toby
1980s, Withington, Herefordshire.

Chapter Sixteen, Page 83
Smith Family Members, 1940s, Herefordshire.

Chapter Seventeen, Page 90
My mother, Elizabeth (Betty) Smith,
with my sister Mary, 1940s Herefordshire.

Chapter Nineteen, Page 98
My uncle and aunt, Tommy and Carol Smith, late 1980s.

Chapter Twenty Three, Page 116
My sister, Mary Haines (nee Smith),
outside the 'water-shed'. Mid 1970s, Yarkhill, Herefordshire.

Chapter Twenty Four, Page 122
My parents, Leonard and Elizabeth Smith, with their neighbours,
1980s, Rudge Grove, Marden, Herefordshire.

Chapter Twenty Six, Page 131
My maternal grandparents, Jeremiah and Rosina Smith
1950s, Weston Beggard, Herefordshire.

Chapter Twenty Eight, Page 137
My uncle Jeremiah (Mushy) Smith with his son,
Jeremiah, 1940s/50s, Worcestershire.

Chapter Twenty Nine, Page 142
Chris Smith and Andrew Tait, 1997,
'Hanging Rock' Victoria, Australia.

Chapter Thirty Two, Page 161
Chris Smith (Walter Brick) and
Les Scarrott (Lez Shed) as Brickshed.
Early 1990s, Mill End Farm, Castle Frome, Herefordshire.

End of Book, Page 175
Smith and Haines family
with Mam's cousins, Dolly and Esther,
late 1970s, Yarkhill, Herefordshire.

End of Book Picture Two, Page 176
Smith/Haines Family
left to right, Chris Smith, Leonard Smith Jnr.
Elizabeth (Betty) Smith, Leonard Smith Snr.
Mary Haines (née Smith),
Front, Nicholas Haines (Mary's Son).
Early 1980s, Yarkhill, Herefordshire.

THE TAN

www.ingramcontent.com/pod-product-compliance
Lightning Source LLC
Chambersburg PA
CBHW050032090426
42735CB00022B/3455